A. WELTGE MD

Division of Emergency Medicine

Avoiding Medical Malpractice

ARTHUR H. BERNSTEIN, J.D.

PLURIBUS PRESS, CHICAGO

©1987 by Pluribus Press,
All Rights Reserved

Except for appropriate use in critical reviews or works of scholarship, the reproduction or use of this work in any form or by any electronic, mechanical or other means now known or hereafter invented, including photocopying and recording, and in any information storage and retrieval system is forbidden without the written permission of the publisher.

Library of Congress Catalog Card Number:
87-60545

International Standard Book Number:
0-931028-91-4

Pluribus Press, Inc.
160 East Illinois Street
Chicago, Illinois 60611

91 90 89 88 87   5 4 3 2 1

Printed in the United States of America

CONTENTS

Introduction / v

Chapter 1—Background / 1

Chapter 2—Psychological Aspects of Malpractice Claims / 21

Chapter 3—Informed Consent / 31

Chapter 4—Diagnostic and Treatment Failures / 69

Chapter 5—Inattention to and Abandonment of Patients / 89

Chapter 6—Personal Problems of Practitioners and Their Employees / 97

Chapter 7—Inhospital Malpractice Prevention / 105

Chapter 8—Reforms in the Legal System and Malpractice Insurance / 141

Chapter 9—Some Parting Advice / 151

Index—155

INTRODUCTION

THIS BOOK was undertaken to demonstrate a simple thesis: If a couple of hundred actual medical malpractice claims were to be examined, they probably would illustrate the gamut of problems encountered in such claims and provide guidance for physicians and hospitals to help prevent similar experiences. Accordingly, various malpractice cases were reviewed. These included those tried before the highest appellate courts, suits that got no further than the initial trial court, cases settled before trial, and claims that were settled prior to filing suit. Additionally, situations reported to insurance carriers by insured physicians and hospitals that never resulted in a suit or claim were examined.

This survey led to the conclusion that real cases, although informative, often are clear-cut and useful for instructional purposes. What they do show, however, is that bad results usually prompt patients to bring these malpractice claims.

Undesired outcomes of the patient-provider encounter are not completely avoidable, or course. The practice of medicine remains an art requiring constant, sometimes fallible judgments. On the other hand, much of the incidence of malpractice *is* avoidable. Avoidance is more likely to the extent that

- Good professional practice is followed.
- Optimal doctor-patient communications occur.
- Accurate, timely medical records are maintained.
- Communications between the physician and his office or the hospital staff are clear and punctual.
- Patients are treated with genuine consideration.
- Physicians do not overstep the bounds of professional ethics.
- Practitioners limit practice to areas of real competence.
- Physicians, impaired because of alcohol, drugs, serious emotional problems, disability, or suffering from deterioration of skills, restrict their practice accordingly.

The book is organized to review briefly the legal concepts of malpractice, the rise of litigation in recent years, the malpractice insurance crisis, and legislative efforts to improve the situation. Most of the volume is devoted to a discussion of particular problem areas, using real case descriptions to illustrate them, with suggestions for ways of avoiding malpractice exposure in these cases.

It should be understood that actual cases disclose only a portion of the causes of malpractice. A lawsuit rarely, if ever, indicates on its face that such factors as a doctor's demeanor, brusqueness, poor communications, aggressive billing practices, unavailability, or excessive charges propelled the patient into court. Thus, many malpractice prevention measures cannot be illustrated by excerpts from claims and lawsuits. Nevertheless, there is general agreement among knowledgeable students of the malpractice field that appropriate behavior is as important, for malpractice avoidance purposes, as professional skills.

The case descriptions presented in this book do not identify the parties involved, the location, the court, or any other facts that might breach confidentiality. This is true whether the case is of public record or is contained in the private files of an insurance company.

Because this is not a text or scientific work, footnotes are intentionally omitted, and few sources of authority are referenced.

The use of the masculine gender throughout this work is intended to refer also to the feminine where appropriate; thus, *his* means *his or her* in most instances.

CHAPTER ONE

Background

IN ORDER TO DERIVE any benefit from this book, the reader must accept the reality that

- Malpractice is being committed with frequency by practitioners and in hospitals.
- A substantial share of the claims is based on provable malpractice.
- Well-trained and well-meaning professionals can commit malpractice, not just quacks, drunks, overreachers, or other recognized poor risks.
- The patient has a right to be well informed and to make his own decisions about his health care, even if, in the view of the provider, they are the wrong ones.

If the reader cannot agree with these basic assumptions, he is unlikely to gain anything from what follows. He simply is not ready to be helped.

Except in a large group-practice setting, there is no one who oversees the office practice of most private practitioners. Here, the individual provider of health care must have sufficient self-discipline to become aware of his risks and to remedy unsafe practices. It is the objective of this book to facilitate this self-education and the remedial action that should follow.

Elements of the Contemporary Scene

Before examining specific situations over which physicians and hospital personnel may have enough control to improve their chances of avoiding medical malpractice liability, it may be helpful to review the contemporary scene and what has led to it.

Professional negligence, which is malpractice, has been a part of American law since the nation was established. The British common law was the basis for the law of "torts," that is, civil (not criminal) personal injury, which includes ordinary negligence and professional negligence. Successful suits by patients against physicians were rare until after World War II, in part because the ability of physicians to diagnose and cure was limited and expectations of their patients were only moderate. Once the medical profession was armed with many effective ways of diagnosing and treating ailments and became a high income group, lawyers became interested in suing for malpractice. It was possible to demonstrate the professional standard of care by qualified expert witnesses, textbooks, or by common knowledge of laymen. It has been said that of all the malpractice actions brought in this country, probably over 90 percent have occurred within the past two decades. Thus, the malpractice situation has been a problem for a comparatively short time.

For hospitals, there was no malpractice risk until the doctrine of sovereign and charitable immunity was dissolved by the various state courts (sometimes by the legislature). Once the courts recognized that hospitals, whether nonprofit, governmental, or investor owned, are businesses that usually charge for their services and should assume responsibility for their negligently injured customers, just as other businesses do, the floodgates opened for malpractice suits against hospitals. This, too, is a serious phenomenon of only about 30 years duration.

ROLE OF INSURANCE

Once both hospitals and doctors were equally exposed to malpractice liability, the task of patients' attorneys was made easier by the sorry spectacle of each defendant trying to save himself by blaming the other, a development that was inevitable as long as the hospitals and their medical staff members were covered by different insurance carriers.

The plaintiff lawyers' successes contributed to rapidly escalating insurance premiums, the departure of many carriers from the field, inability of some providers to obtain or afford malpractice insurance, and voluntary restriction or termination of practice by some specialists. To all providers, the high cost of insurance meant charging increased fees. Possibly the worst effect of all was the developing apprehension about certain patients by physicians due to fear of potential litigation. Defensive medicine became standard practice, and the costs of health care escalated even more steeply as a result.

Because the most serious malpractice claims arise out of inhospital cases, many hospitals require that their medical staff members have adequate insurance protection. For the hospitals, corporate liability may occur if the peer review process is inadequate to protect the public from unqualified or incompetent physicians on the staff. Thus, the hospital must have an ongoing screening process to ensure that its doctors are practicing at acceptable levels of professional skill. Risk management programs also try to detect substandard performance and to institute necessary corrective measures within the institution.

The "deep-pocket" principle, as recognized in many states, presents a further threat to hospitals. If there is a verdict for the patient against a hospital and several doctors, and "joint and several" liability applies, each defendant is potentially liable for the entire judgment if other codefendants cannot pay their share. Lack of insurance or assets by the doctors who are responsible by virtue of a jury assessment for, say, 90 percent of the liability, may mean that the insured hospital will pay all of the judgment despite a finding that it was only 10 percent liable. It is no wonder, then, that some hospitals insist that all medical staff members be properly insured.

MALPRACTICE REFORM LAWS

Corrective legislation pertaining to malpractice has been adopted in many states at the behest of organized medicine and hospitals. California has been the leader in this endeavor to cut the cost of losing malpractice cases and to make them less attractive to patients and their lawyers. It has taken 10 years for California's Supreme Court to rule on all features of the tort reform statute, upholding them and thereby encouraging similar laws in other states. These measures require awards of future damages beyond $50,000 to be disbursed in periodic payments; allow introduction of evidence that the patient's medical and other damages were paid by a third party; limit plaintiffs' attorneys' contingent fee schedules; and restrict awards for pain and suffering to $250,000. In 1986, the voters of California approved a measure that partially closes the "deep pocket" by holding jointly liable defendants to only their proportionate share of noneconomic (pain and suffering) damages.

It should be noted that the impact of the California malpractice tort reforms has been to reduce the amount paid out in cases involving large awards and to curtail plaintiffs' attorneys' fees in those instances. However, the number of cases filed against doctors and hospitals has not been reduced and the average award has continued to climb (although possibly at a reduced rate). Therefore, tort reform provides no justification for relaxation of efforts to deter those situations that could lead to malpractice claims. The statutory reforms may well have assured the continued availability of malpractice insurance, albeit at a steep price.

Recent Statistics on Malpractice

As bad as the malpractice situation may seem, it would be an absolute catastrophe if all or most "compensable events" resulted in claims. Careful surveys by competent physician-lawyers have led to a shocking conclusion—that the number of cases of apparently provable malpractice, judged by examining hospital records, is many times the number of actual claims. Instead of a populace made up of litigious scoundrels, it appears that most patients who have suffered because of probable malpractice are not aware of it, would rather not bother with litigation, or wait too long to take action and are barred by the statute of limitations. If such is the case, a genuinely alert patient population, acting on their suspicions of malpractice by suing, could very well destroy the private health care delivery system of the United States. This is all the more reason to prevent avoidable malpractice.

That a small percentage of "rotten apple" physicians cause most of the problem is belied by the statistics. In 1975, 8.5 doctors per thousand were sued. By 1984, it was 16.4. Obviously, that is far in excess of the number of rotten apples in the profession. It also constitutes a doubling of the incidence of suits. In a similar 10-year period, the average malpractice award has tripled. Depending upon the source of data, the average jury award now may be close to $1 million. Insurance premiums have increased as well. Horror stories abound of New York neurosurgeons paying premiums of over $125,000, obstetricians $100,000, and orthopedists $80,000 for a year's coverage.

The impact of very high insurance premiums is both beneficial and harmful to the public. Practitioners who are not confident of all of their skills have chosen to stop doing some procedures. That may be a public service. However, when useful community physicians decide to retire prematurely or give up delivering babies, the public may be deprived of necessary care because of unaffordable malpractice insurance premiums. Particularly affected are doctors who would prefer to practice part time but discover the premium is almost as much as what they might earn.

The making of a malpractice claim does not mean that malpractice has occurred, of course. Nevertheless, malpractice insurers have indicated that, after investigation, they conclude that about two-thirds of the claims have merit. These include iatrogenic illnesses. A lesser percentage of claims are compensated because, in many instances, while there may have been negligence, there may not have been significant enough injury as a direct consequence of the negligence.

COST OF LAWYERS

A word about the role of lawyers in the malpractice process: Admittedly, they siphon off too much of the money involved. Between the patients' lawyers and the defense counsel, a majority of the malpractice insurance premiums is absorbed. Deduct the carriers' administrative cost and profit, if any, and it is clear that the injured patient is a lesser beneficiary of the funds expended.

To be sure, aggressive plaintiffs' attorneys have managed to win cases by means of novel legal theories, and their successes have induced more patients to try their luck in the malpractice sweepstakes. But what is little known outside of the plaintiffs' bar is the selectivity of malpractice attorneys. Those who have proven records in this legal specialty, and who serve patients on a contingent fee basis, do not accept clients whose cases are not likely to be won. And attorneys who are not experienced in handling malpractice suits have poor prospects for winning. Obviously, no lawyer is willing to work for nothing, which is the consequence of losing a case for which the plaintiff owes no fee if there is no award of damages.

One survey showed that malpractice lawyers reject at least 71 percent of cases presented to them. Reasons for declining representation of unhappy patients or their survivors include no perceived liability (41%), case not worthwhile economically (10%), and difficulty of proving malpractice even if convinced that it occurred (5%). Once an experienced malpractice attorney decides to accept a case, his likelihood of obtaining some payment is almost 80 percent. Tort reform legislation that reduces attorney contingent fees on larger awards and limits some kinds of damages and the total awards on which the attorney's percentage is based do not seem to have reduced the availability of qualified attorneys to bring malpractice actions.

CLAIMS EXPERIENCE

The interrelationship of doctors and hospitals is an interesting malpractice phenomenon. Most malpractice claims arise in the hospital setting—about three-fourths of them. In almost all of these cases, one or more physicians is sued. In fact, a physician usually is the primary defendant. The results are payments in these situations by or on behalf of physicians averaging 70 percent of the award and by hospitals of 25 percent. (Nurses, dentists, and others make up the balance.)

For hospitals, data are presented in terms of the frequency of malpractice claims per 100 beds. California experience shows that claims rose from 1.60 to 3 per 100 beds from 1974 to 1983. Average cost per claim (whether successful or not) rose in the same period from $4,800 to $12,785. However, when one examines the performance of California juries in litigated malpractice cases, one finds that the average amount awarded per claim, if an award was made, rose from $200,000 in 1972 to $650,000 in 1983. It is clear that many small claims are being settled, with or without payment, outside the courtroom.

California law requires that a report be made to a state agency whenever a settlement or award in excess of a statutory sum is made in response to a malpractice claim. For hospital claims, these rose from an average of $41,000 in 1978 to $103,000 in 1984. All of the California figures presumably reflect the restraining influences of the malpractice reform statute.

REASONS FOR CLAIMS

What do the surveys reveal about the bad results for which patients make malpractice claims? One report covering the years 1975-78 included these asserted causes: improperly performed procedures, 35 percent; diagnostic errors, 27 percent; and drug-related injuries, 10 percent. Only 2 to 3 percent of claims paid were for permanent or disabling injuries, but these, along with anesthesia misadventures, were very costly.

A 1981 report on the Michigan experience showed which medical specialties were the most frequent targets of malpractice claims. General surgery was the easy winner, followed by general practice, internal medicine, and orthopedic surgery.

The gross frequency of claims in any specialty is not directly proportional to the cost. California insurance carriers' statistics for 1970-73, for example, show how much more was paid out than received in premiums for the various specialties. Thus, family practice produced a loss ratio of 269 (based on 100 as the break-even point); thoracic surgery, 260; colon and rectal surgery, 255; neurological surgery, 251; general practice with no surgery, 205; and internal medicine with no surgery, 214. More recently, neurosurgeons and obstetricians have moved to the top of the list. To the insurers, these were the most disappointing specialities.

Another report from a malpractice carrier lists the percentage of claims against physicians by major categories. Half the malpractice suits are based upon allegations of improper treatment. A quarter assert failure to properly diagnose. And 11 percent stem from bad results of surgery. Thus, the remaining identified problem areas make up only about 15 percent of the number of claims. At the top of this list is anesthesia, followed in descending order by informed consent, injection site injury, emotional trauma, abandonment, failure to refer, transfusions, radiation burns, failure to offer alternative treatment, and billing difficulties.

Presented another way, the leading causes of claims (not the amount of compensation) were found to be surgical error, lack of supervision or control of assistants, postoperative surgical complications, failure to detect fracture, improper treatment of fracture or relocation, birth-related problems, drug side effects, failure to diagnose cancer, infection, and informed consent. This list indicates that suits arise both from failure of professional skill or judgment and of communication. Evidently, malpractice has a technical and psychological component. Each is amenable to alteration in the quest for lowering malpractice claims to the irreducible minimum.

One Insurer's Experience, 1981-85

The following charts, provided by the St. Paul Fire and Marine Insurance Co., the leading insurer of hospitals and physicians in the United States, indicate the growth of the number of claims against physicians and hospitals between 1981 and 1985, in payments to settle malpractice claims, and for administration of those claims (mostly defense legal costs) during the same period. Also included is a chart comparing the number of claims per 100 insured doctors in 1981 and 1985 by type of practice (insurance class rating). The first of two final charts identifies malpractice claims filed in 1984 and 1985 against physicians by the type of alleged injury, categorized alternatively by number of claims, average cost of claims, and location of the incident. The second chart gives similar information about malpractice claims against hospitals for the same period.

Physician and Surgeon Claim Experience
Cumulative Increase Since 1981

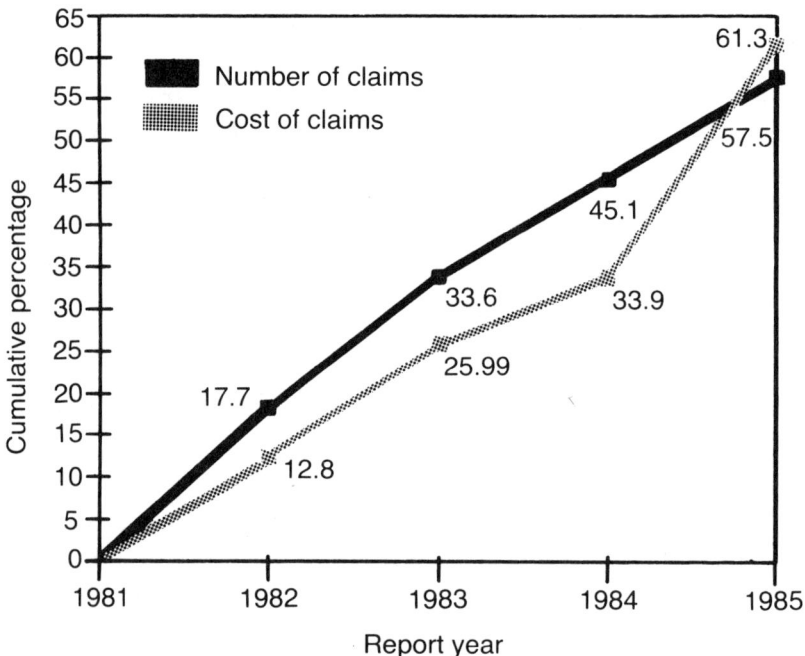

Both the cost and number of professional liability claims against St. Paul-insured physicians and surgeons continue to climb at alarming rates. Rises in claim frequency averaged 12 percent per year since 1981. Claim severity for losses up to $100,000 rose an average of 13 percent per year over the same period. The combined effect of these claim frequency and severity trends is an average annual rise of 26 percent for physician and surgeon countrywide loss costs, 41 percent in 1985 alone.

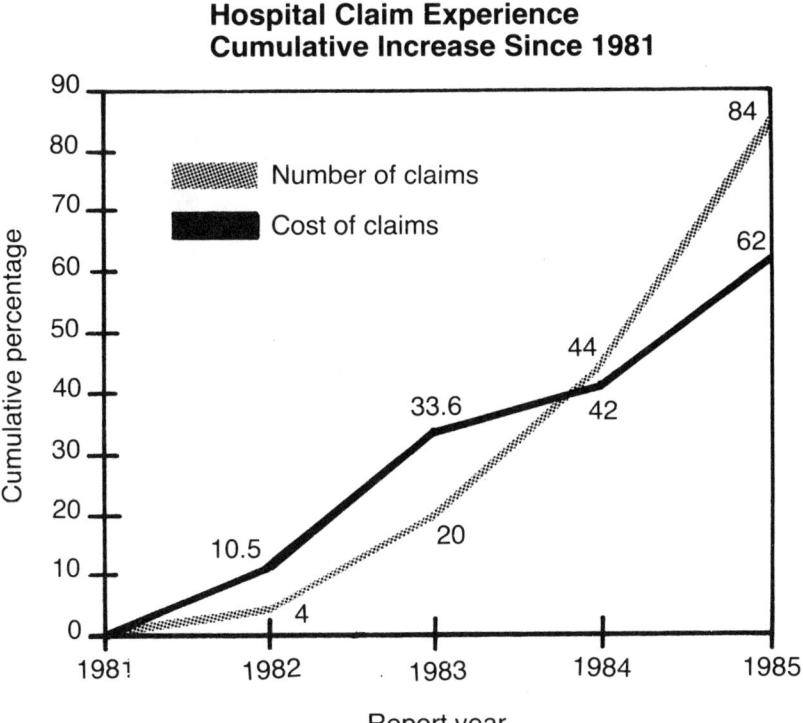

Both the cost and number of professional liability claims against St. Paul-insured hospitals continue to climb at alarming rates. Rises in claim frequency averaged nearly 17 percent per year since 1981. The cost per claim (capped at $100,000) rose an average of 13 percent per year over the same period. The combined effect of these claim frequency and severity trends is an average annual rise of nearly 32 percent for hospital countrywide loss costs, more that 45 percent in 1985 alone.

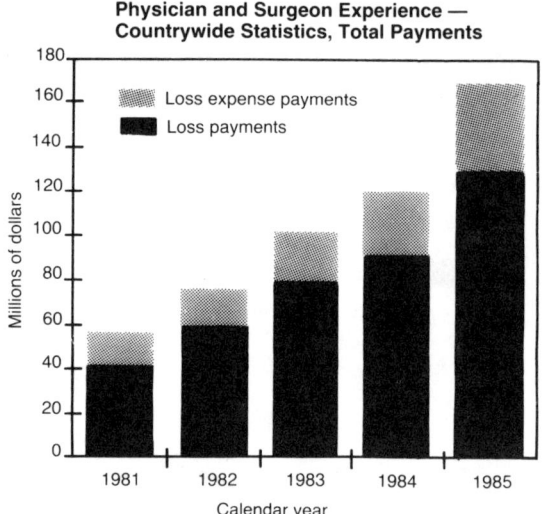

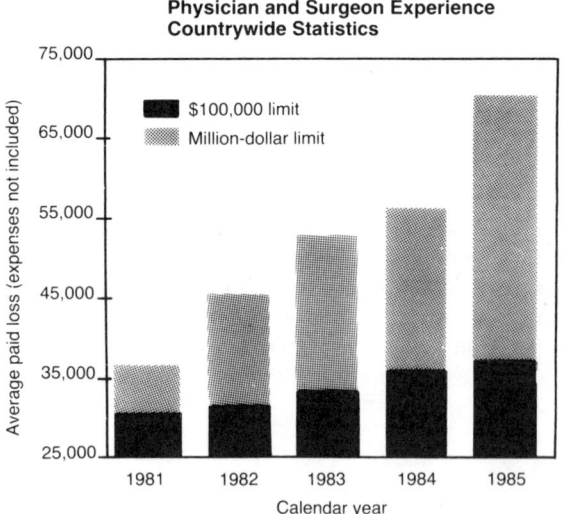

BACKGROUND

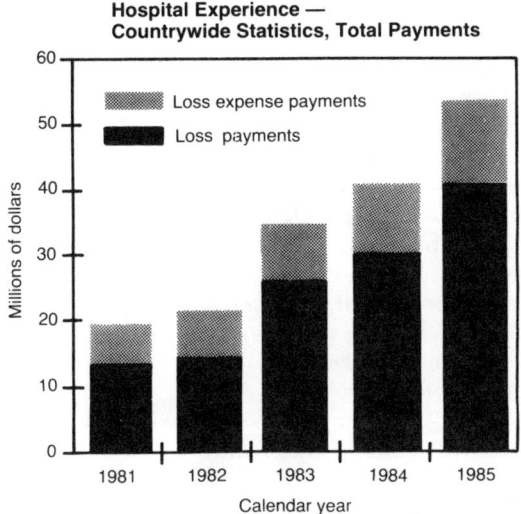

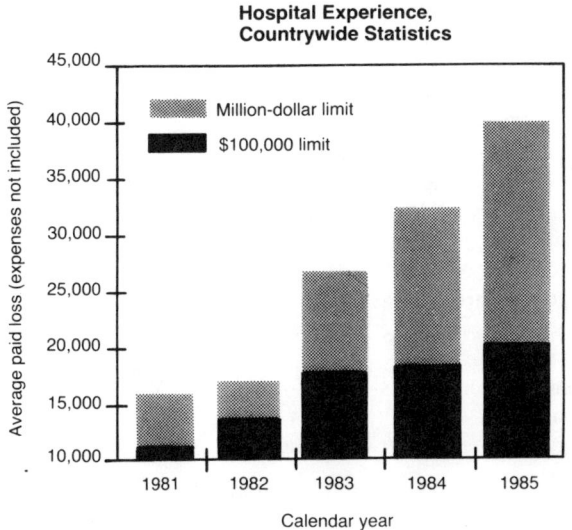

Comparison of Malpractice Claims Against Physicians, 1981 and 1985, by Type of Practice

Insurance rating class	Specialty definition	Number of claims (per 100 doctors)		
		1981	1985	% increase
1	Physicians—no surgery, no invasive procedures, no obstetrical procedures	4.6	9.2	100
2	Physicians—minor surgery, minor invasive procedures, no obstetrical procedures	6.9	12.7	84
3	Family or General Practice—including obstetrical procedures (excluding cesarean sections)/Urgent Care Physician—no surgery/Bronco-esophagology/Physicians—major invasive procedures/Surgery—colon and rectal, endocrinology, gastroenterology, geriatrics, neoplastic, nephrology, ophthamology and urological	9.4	14.2	51
4	Family or General Practice—major surgery/Emergency Medicine—no major surgery	16.7	19.9	19
5a.	Anesthesiologist	11.1	17.8	60
5	Emergency Medicine—major surgery/Surgery—abdominal, general, gynecology, hand, head and neck, laryngology, otology, otorhinolaryngology, plastic, plastic—otorhinolaryngology and rhinology	19.9	25.5	28
6	Surgery—cardiac, cardiovascular, orthopedic, thoracic, traumatic and vascular	24.8	36.9	49
7	Obstetrics/Obstetrics—Gynecology	27.5	43.7	59
8	Surgery—Neurological (including child)	30.8	50.1	63

Summary of 1984-85 Malpractice Claims Against St. Paul-Insured Physicians

By frequency

Allegation	Number	Average cost*
1. Surgery/post-op complications	1,760	$39,998
2. Improper treatment/birth-related	804	91,350
3. Failure to diagnose/cancer	631	70,544
4. Surgery/inadvertent act	571	47,421
5. Failure to diagnose/fracture-dislocation	452	34,311
6. Improper treatment/drug side effect	425	38,905
7. Surgery/inappropriate procedure	414	41,471
8. Failure to diagnose/pregnancy problems	364	56,690
9. Improper treatment/fracture-dislocation	344	32,654
10. Failure to diagnose/infection	300	77,979

By average cost**

Allegation	Number	Average cost*
1. Anesthesia/cardiac arrest	129	$115,672
2. Anesthesia/catastrophic undescribed	106	108,144
3. Improper treatment/birth-related	804	91,350
4. Failure to diagnose/hemorrhage	96	78,720
5. Failure to diagnose infection	300	77,979
6. Surgery/post-op death	243	74,035
7. Failure to diagnose/cancer	631	70,544
8. Failure to diagnose/myocardial infarction	164	67,241
9. Failure to diagnose/circulatory problem	149	64,524
10. Failure to diagnose/pregnancy problems	364	56,690

By location

Location	Number	Average cost*
Physician's office	2,647	$41,420
Clinic	1,203	36,927
Surgicenter	112	46,555
Hospital—all areas	9,071	50,307
Emergency room	1,255	45,169
Operating room	4,374	45,752
Obstetrics	1,060	89,173
Patient care area	1,607	49,857
Outpatient surgery	152	47,386
Other areas	623	28,390

*Average cost includes the total value of the claim, including allocated legal expense and no cap on individual claims. The average reflects all claims reported from 1984-85, including those closed without payment, evaluated as of 3/86.

**The Top 10 ranking for claim severity is based on the average cost of loss for allegations resulting in 95 reported claims or more.

Summary of 1984-85 Malpractice Claims Against St. Paul-Insured Hospitals

By location	Number	Average cost*
Patient care (nursing)	2,419	$22,044
Inpatient surgery	1,523	20,503
Emergency	1,365	20,312
Obstetrics	773	66,834
Outpatient surgery	194	14,424
Psychiatric services	184	29,608
Radiology	169	11,484
Outpatient services	167	16,693
Therapy services	97	16,747

By frequency	Number	Average cost*
1. Treatment complications/bad results	531	$29,000
2. Treatment (delayed or omitted)	498	43,426

3. Fall (bed-related)	371	11,654
4. Treatment (adjacent injury	344	16,787
5. Wrong diagnosis	321	22,754
6. Incorrect treatment	318	26,705
7. Treatment (infection/contamination/exposure)	313	22,825
8. Other treatment issues	312	25,083
9. Diagnosis (misinterpreted results of HPT**)	242	21,461
10. Fall (ambulation-related)	237	10,807

By severity	Number	Average cost*
1. Treatment (patient monitoring-related)	156	$71,358
2. Diagnosis (omitted HPT**)	45	51,960
3. Treatment (omitted or delayed)	498	43,426
4. Treatment (amount/rate incorrect/unordered)	179	40,193
5. Diagnosis (delayed HPT**)	128	39,402
6. Treatment (intubation-related)	63	39,987
7. Diagnosis (improperly performed HPT**)	127	37,866
8. Self-inflicted injury/suicide	64	36,063
9. Malfunction/failure of facility/equipment	102	36,037
10. Lack of adequate facility/equipment	15	35,156

*Average cost includes the total value of the claim, including allocated legal expense and no cap on individual claims. The average reflects all claims reported from 1984-85, including those closed without payment, evaluated as of 6/86. Total cost is the product of the average cost and the total number of claims.

**HPT: History/physical/diagnostic testing.

Some Definitions

Before proceeding to attack the remediable causes of malpractice, some definitions are in order. Malpractice is the failure by a professional to exercise an accepted degree of professional skill or learning. It is actionable only if it is the proximate cause of injury, loss, or damage. A general physician must exercise the degree of care, skill, and diligence that is used by ordinarily careful physicians in similar circumstances in like communities. However, specialists are held to a national standard of competence. In order to present a compensable case at law, the patient must show that he was injured as a result of substandard professional care and that such care was a contributing cause of the injury. Thus, without injury, even substandard care—professional malpractice—should not be compensable.

It should be borne in mind that a physician is not held to the highest degree of care or skill or judgment, but rather to just an ordinary level. Nor is he a guarantor of cures unless he promises to achieve a particular desired result.

Most malpractice cases require expert testimony, by qualified professional witnesses, to prove that the professional care was substandard. Until fairly recently, few physicians were available to so testify, leading to the accusation of a professional "conspiracy of silence." Today, professional witnesses are widely available, constituting an unofficial subspecialty. Laymen also may testify as to malpractice, but only for common situations that require no professional knowledge to identify substandard care.

If there are two or more professionally accepted methods of handling a medical problem, choosing one over another is not malpractice. Specialists, of course, are held to a higher degree of skill than are general practitioners. And of itself, a bad result is not evidence of, nor does it presume that there was, malpractice.

Malpractice is a tort, a civil but not a criminal wrong. It is usually governed by state law, which does differ from one jurisdiction to another. Therefore, these comments are general and not specific to any particular state unless so noted.

A word about damages, the end result of an unsuccessful defense of a malpractice suit: Who may be compensated? Not only the injured patient, but a spouse, dependent relatives, and a deceased patient's estate. What are special damages? These include past, present, and future medical expenses of the patient, lost earnings, or impaired earning capacity. What "nonpecuniary" damages may be awarded? General damages include those for pain and suffering, a very subjective matter over which juries are given broad discretion. May punitive damages be awarded in medical malpractice cases? Yes. Intentionally harmful, malicious, or grossly negligent defendants may be punished by award of damages over and above compensatory damages "to teach them a lesson" and deter repetition of the egregious professional misconduct.

Malpractice that causes the patient's death gives rise to a wrongful death claim by surviving dependent relatives. However, there can be no punitive damages or awards for grief, sorrow, or mental suffering in wrongful death claims. Additionally, separate damages can be awarded to a spouse who suffered "loss of consortium" because of a negligent injury to the patient. Finally, a growing area of damages is for negligent infliction of emotional distress upon members of the patient's family who actually observe or are seriously affected by the negligent act.

Ordinarily, the older the injured patient, the less the life expectancy and the lower the damage award. Similarly, the high-earning patient's lost earnings will bring more economic damages than those of a lesser earner.

Summary

1. A great many more malpractice incidents occur in office practice and hospitals than are the subject of malpractice claims and suits.

2. Whatever success "ambulance chasing" attorneys may have in inducing otherwise unknowing or unwilling patients to make malpractice claims is a minor consideration in the light of the massive incidence of "potentially compensable events" not acted upon. Lawyers reject most would-be malpractice plaintiffs.

3. Perhaps one of every 20 hospitalized patients incurs an iatrogenic injury. Far fewer make claims.

4. Bad results usually are the initial basis for litigation, but how the patient and family are treated may determine whether a claim will be pursued.

5. Communications—effectively conveyed information—between doctor and patient and between physician and office and hospital personnel are the key factor in most preventable malpractice claims situations.

6. Insurance carriers are not very much interested in the medical malpractice risk business because they have been paying out far more in claims than they have received in recent years, amounts not always made up by their investment income.

7. Tort reform may reduce the size of the larger awards and thus encourage malpractice insurers to remain in the field, but it is unlikely that it will significantly lower the number or cost of middle range claims, which represent a major problem.

8. Malpractice risk extends to well-trained and usually careful practitioners. Some instances are unavoidable, others reflect overwork or laxity, and some are the consequence of poor communications. The latter two categories are the remedial ones.

9. Patients rarely sue a doctor considered to be a caring personal friend who devotes adequate time and attention to the patient's perceived needs and is honest in communicating with the patient.

CHAPTER TWO

Psychological Aspects of Malpractice Claims

ALTHOUGH in almost all malpractice cases the patient has had an unsatisfactory result of professional care, many such injuries do not lead to litigation. Aside from those patients who are ignorant of their rights, there are those who are aware of both their injury and the possibility of suit who forgo suing because of the way the physician and hospital personnel have communicated with the patient and family members.

An untoward result of medical treatment need not lead to a plaintiffs' attorney's office if there has been good rapport with the patient. Considerate care, featuring frank disclosure, sympathetic concern, and respect for the patient's dignity, will go a long way in dissuading a patient from seeking an attorney's services. On the other hand, the overly busy physician who appears disinterested in the patient's problem or has written off the patient as of no further interest is inviting the patient's negative reaction. Continuing concern for the patient, expressed with warmth, may well exceed all the powers of insurers and their legal counsel for defending or preventing malpractice claims.

Genuine Concern as a Preventive

Examples have been recorded of patients who have been dismissed by physicians, sometimes as needing a psychiatrist rather than an internist, and who are later diagnosed as having a serious physical ailment. These patients are psychologically ready to seek a litigation solution to their hurt feelings. Similarly, the physician who presses patients for payment with continuing physical problems is ripe for retaliation. By inquiring of the patient's condition before pursuing aggressive collection procedures, a faux pas may be avoided.

Just letting the patient know about his medical condition often is enough to allay the patient's apprehensions. A routine follow-up phone call from time to time could be all that is required to satisfy the patient's personal concern and to reassure him that the doctor cares about him and is providing all the information he needs. Certainly, it takes the doctor's valuable time to do this, but it may prove to be an outstanding investment if it precludes malpractice litigation.

WARNING OF DISCOMFORT

Anticipating adverse reactions or just the discomfort of a normal recovery is the doctor's obligation. He should advise the patient, without frightening him, about these possibilities. Otherwise, the patient may blame the doctor for not having enough skill to prevent the discomfort. The patient, in fact, may consider the unpleasantness the result of malpractice just because the doctor failed to warn of it.

The medical office staff must be trained to avoid screening patient calls to the doctor to the extent that the patient feels cut off from his practitioner. Eventually, the patient may not call when he should, and any ensuing bad result could lead to malpractice litigation because the patient believes that the physician has virtually abandoned him. This is especially the risk when the staff classifies a patient as a pest, a hypochondriac, or a neurotic. Even disturbed people may have real physical problems.

Once it is clear that malpractice has occurred, it is best not to cover up the reality of what happened. Half-truths, incomplete disclosure of facts, and blaming others will only assure a lawsuit once the patient becomes aware that he has been victimized by negligence. Defense attorneys tell of cases where a foreign object has been left in a patient after a surgical procedure, a mistake that cannot be defended in court, and because the patient was given quick and truthful disclosure and corrective care, he opted not to seek damages from the surgeon.

Sources of Dissatisfaction

A survey of California patients in 1984 indicated that the areas of least satisfaction had to do with explanations to patients. They were particularly unhappy with what they were told of drug side effects, postprocedure pain, description and reporting of the patient's condition, and the cost of the treatment or procedure. Discussion of alternative treatment and need for postsurgical reassurance also were high on the patients' lists. Also, when referred to a surgeon, patients were unclear as to whom to contact. They had not been apprised of the responsibilities of the respective physicians.

Only a few patients are cold and calculating, looking upon a good malpractice suit as a fine way to acquire money without working (and usually tax free). More commonly, the patient must consider himself to have had a bad result and then come to the conclusion that it should not have happened that way. If the patient also feels abandoned, or disappointed or angry with his doctor, the preconditions for a malpractice claim exist.

Anger toward a physician may be the result of overreliance upon him. Elevating a doctor to the status of a deity is fine as long as there are no bad results, but the medical god who fails is not immune from suit. Many patients encourage physicians to play God, but the wise practitioner will remind the patient of the mortal origins of doctors.

DOCTOR-PATIENT RELATIONSHIP

A highly personal relationship between patient and doctor is not readily maintained in big institutions, large medical groups, or in other depersonalized settings. It is in these situations that doctor-patient communications are most likely to fail. Obviously, an impersonal relationship between patient and physician is more common in large organizations, although not unavoidable, and the psychological ingredients for litigation are more readily developed there. Both lawyers and physicians have written that a malpractice suit resembles a divorce or lovers' breakup. The disappointed patient, having had strong feelings about the doctor—even entrusting him with his life—feels heightened animosity. The greater the patient's feelings of trust toward the doctor, the more intense the anger over the disillusionment. If this psychological conundrum can be solved, the answer must grow from having the patient perceive the physician realistically and forcing the patient to make decisions about his medical care rather than relying unquestioningly upon the physician to do so.

Somehow, the patient must be made to realize that there are risks in the contemplated procedure, or possibilities of a failed diagnosis or adverse side effects, and that those risks apply to him, not just to others. While a confident patient is desirable, one who expects nothing short of a perfect outcome could be easily converted into a malpractice plaintiff if results do not meet his expectations. Because they sometimes equate a bad result with error, the patient's family members should be included in the explanation of realistic expectations.

Unanticipated High Bills

For those patients who must pay for all or part of their medical expenses, disputed bills can trigger enough dissatisfaction to prompt a lawyer's investigation of possible malpractice. If the doctor is aware of an unsatisfactory result of care—and he should inquire of the patient to ascertain this—he should avoid persistent billing and collection efforts until he has had an opportunity to talk with or see the patient. But prior to treatment, upon learning that the patient is personally liable for costs, the physician should raise the question of money and try to estimate the cost of treatment. When the bills significantly exceed that figure, the physician should contact the patient and explain the reasons. Granted, this takes away valuable practice time, but maintaining good communications with the patient is not only a good preventive for malpractice claims, it is an integral part of the practice of medicine. The doctor-patient relationship includes necessary communication, not just technical services.

Careful Instructions and Follow-up

One psychologist, after inquiring into the doctor-patient relationship, discovered that only about 10 percent of hospitalized patients who might have sued for malpractice actually do so. The difference found between those who sue and those who do not often stems from the relationship between provider and patient. The patient must have trust in the physician. Full explanation of what to expect and what the patient must do will help the physician build this necessary respect. Explicit, repeated instructions to the patient are essential, even if they are just common sense, and in the physician's view, patients already know about. In fact, the psychologist suggested that physicians ask each patient to write out his questions as a way of eliciting what the patient does not understand. If the patient has seen more than one physician in an organization, or has been referred to a specialist, it would be well for the primary physician to summarize the findings for the patient. Although it may seem to be a luxury, a follow-up telephone call or letter after each visit or series of tests, or upon conclusion of an episode of care, may create the kind of attitude toward the physician that discourages litigation. It may permit discovery of patient dissatisfaction and prevent continuation of a smoldering resentment. Alternatively, the patient may be instructed to call back at certain intervals to report on his condition. By showing that the provider cares about the patient, positive patient attitudes may be encouraged, thus reducing the risk of malpractice claims.

Practice By Telephone

Something as basic as telephone behavior can influence patient attitudes sufficiently to affect the incidence of malpractice claims. Diagnosing, treating, and prescribing over the phone is commonly done and is unavoidable. Nevertheless, there is an inherent malpractice risk whenever the physician acts without seeing the patient. The legally recognized doctor-patient relationship prevails whether the physician sees the patient or relies upon telephoning information instead. Therefore, if there is any doubt in the mind of the physician, he should insist upon examining the patient rather than relying upon the telephone to impart information. To the extent that the source of information is not the patient, diagnosing and prescribing based on untrained second-hand observers becomes a greater risk.

Telephone conversations can be misunderstood. Consequently, the physician must not only try to be clear, ascertaining whether the message has been properly understood, perhaps by having the instructions repeated back to the doctor, but he also should make a written notation of what was said. The same applies to orders telephoned to the hospital.

Upon the next visit to the hospital, the physican should check on the accuracy of the medical record entry of the telephoned order.

Patients should be able to reach the physician's office, if not the physician directly, at all reasonable hours. If it is necessary to place the caller on "hold," this should be done only after he has stated the purpose of the call. A system for conveying such call information to the physician promptly is essential so that the patients may be called back in the order of the urgency of their problems. The physician who impresses the patient as being unavailable, slow to respond to calls, or curt in his responses is vulnerable to a suit-minded patient when a bad result occurs.

Who Said What

To be sure, a physician cannot really know how much the patient is absorbing when explanations are given. Despite a comprehensive and clear presentation about the patient's problem, diagnosis, suggested treatment, alternative choices of care, and prognosis, the patient may not have absorbed it all, may reject the reality of it, or may soon forget most of it. Patients "turn off" under varying circumstances. Somehow, the physician must try to detect this, because the patient may later deny that he was told of various risks and the alternatives, confident that he is telling the truth. In court, an injured patient confronting a physician in a contest of memories may be the more persuasive to the jury. Hence, it is imperative for the physician to make notes or recordings to demonstrate what he told the patient.

In addition, a patient who shuts down his receptors or who is selective in hearing what the doctor is saying must be handled in a special manner. A patient shocked upon hearing that he has a dread disease may hear nothing else thereafter and may have no questions at that time. The physician will have to volunteer questions for the patient, or quiz the patient, in order to determine what he has understood. Presenting the patient with a written statement as to diagnosis, treatment options, and prognosis, instructing him to read it and call back soon thereafter, may help to get the full message through to the patient (and his family). The story should be repeated subsequently, perhaps involving other health care providers, in order to ensure its absorption. In all these presentations, there must be a conscious effort to use commonly understood terms rather than technical language. Laymen rarely are familiar with anatomy and diagnostic terminology, although they may be ashamed to admit it. Therefore, they will nod affirmatively when asked if they understand, revealing their lack of comprehension only if asked to restate the information. Having a companion accompany the patient may assist the learning process and help allay future misunderstanding that could lead to a malpractice claim.

Accepting Fallibility

Psychological considerations concerning malpractice claims should be examined not only with regard to patients who may bring suit if preconditioned to do so but also in relation to the physicians who may be sued. Many physicians are unable to admit to their errors of judgment or performance. This may not be solely the problem of individual personalities. Possibly, it is the very nature of medical training and the highly respected position of physicians in our society that make it difficult for some doctors to accept their inadequacies. Intensive medical school programs, exhaustive hospital residencies, and the lack of peer review in most private practice settings leave little opportunity for reflection on professional frailties. If the doctor expects himself to be right almost all the time, and was trained to be, it will be hard to acknowledge error and to take remedial measures. How much easier it is to blame others. This counterproductive behavior often facilitates proof of malpractice and guarantees an award to the injured plaintiff. It is likely to lead to defensive attitudes, apprehension about patients' motives, and a worsening doctor-patient relationship—all ingredients in the malpractice mix.

The physician who accepts the facts—that good doctors sometimes commit malpractice, and that some malpractice can be avoided through personal carefulness, and that many claims may be deterred by good doctor-patient communications—can take steps to reduce his exposure to malpractice claims. In so doing, his own confidence will be enhanced and his insurance premiums may be contained. In addition, the patient should benefit—something that health care providers also desire.

CHAPTER THREE

Informed Consent

THE LIST of reasons given for making malpractice claims rarely has a category for poor communications between doctor and patient. Yet, many of the claims would not have been pursued had there not been inadequate rapport between provider and patient. In one legal classification, however, failed communication *is* the offense. That is "informed consent."

Only within the past few decades has the law made clear the physician's responsibility to reveal to the patient all that is needed in order to make an informed decision as to whether to receive treatment and, if so, what particular procedures are to be done. No longer does "the doctor know best." In fact, only in special circumstances may the patient toss the burden of decision-making back to the doctor—in true emergencies and when the mental state of the patient precludes his enduring a full explanation of the procedure, its alternatives and the risks associated with it.

Oral and Written Consent

The requirement of informed consent stems from assault and battery statutes and from the constitutional right of privacy enjoyed by all Americans. Their bodies may not be touched or invaded without their consent except in a dire emergency or if they are unconscious. To be sure, most simple procedures have carried implied consent, such as when a doctor examines a patient, inoculates him, takes an x-ray, or sets a broken bone. However, invasive procedures, other than simple diagnostic tests, and other treatments that have a potential for harm if something goes wrong, require specific consent. This may be oral or written. Oral consent is valid, but it is hard to prove. Once the patient has incurred a bad result, his memory may conveniently wipe out the oral presentation. Even with good intentions, the patient is unlikely to remember most of what the doctor told him. Nor will the physician really recall his presentation a few years later when questioned under oath. Therefore, a written consent form, if properly structured, helps to provide a record of the patient's consent. The consent form, primarily a document for the legal protection of the physician (and hospital), also serves to educate the patient.

Obtaining Informed Consent

The consent form itself is not "informed consent." It is only evidence of a written presentation signed by the patient or his parent or legal guardian. To be informed, a consent must be based upon sufficient information and understanding on the part of the patient. This can be accomplished entirely by a written statement, but that is uncommon. A conversation between physician and patient (not the office assistant or admitting clerk) usually is essential for obtaining and proving informed consent. The doctor is expected to speak in terms the patient can understand and elicit questions from the patient to test his comprehension. The patient should be given time to think about all he has heard and ask further questions subsequently (short of a genuine urgency to commence treatment).

It must be emphasized that the mere possession of a consent form signed by the patient and recollection of a proper conversation between patient and physician are not always sufficient to defend against a charge of failure to obtain informed consent. The discussion is critical. In order to prove that the doctor made a complete presentation of all the patient needed to know in order to make an intelligent decision, the doctor must either record the conversation or make complete notes in the patient's medical record of what was covered in the discussion. This notation must be entered soon after the presentation or else it may be suspect.

No Informed Consent vs. No Consent At All

Admittedly, time spent in trying to educate patients so they will be able to make sound decisions in consenting to medical care must be subtracted from the time available to the physician to provide useful treatment. But educating patients is a legally recognized component of medical care; that is, failure to obtain informed consent is malpractice, or medical negligence, and the penalties are similar to those for any substandard professional care. Failure to obtain any consent at all is a worse offense. It may constitute assault and battery. Then, all that the patient need prove in court is that there was no consent, the physician treated the patient, and there was a resulting injury. It is not necessary for the patient to show professional error, lack of skill in conducting the medical procedure, or to call in expert witnesses.

About a quarter of all medical malpractice suits involve alleged failure to obtain informed consent. In most such cases, the patient also claims that there was other malpractice as well. Not uncommon is the situation in which the physician is able to prove that there was no malpractice in treatment but the jury finds an absence of informed consent and awards damages anyway for the patient's bad result. In most instances, these are preventable awards, since obtaining and proving informed consent rarely is an impossibility.

There are many nuisances in the practice of medicine, and, in the doctor's view, obtaining informed consent may be one of them. There is no escape, however. But rather than being viewed as a tiresome obligation, obtaining informed consent can be regarded as an opportunity to improve the doctor-patient relationship, to better understand the patient's viewpoint, and as a test of the doctor's ability to communicate understandably with laymen.

Content of Disclosure

What must the doctor tell the patient? The answer is, just what a reasonable person in the patient's position would want and need to know, especially about the risks of unfavorable results or side effects. Usually, this encompasses a description of the contemplated procedure itself, the probable outcome, and the risks associated with the procedure and with alternative procedures or treatments. The doctor must not forget to discuss the option of having no procedure at all and the consequences of this decision.

Only in special situations should the physician avail himself of the "therapeutic privilege" of refraining from making full disclosure to the patient because it might adversely affect the patient's physical or emotional state. To rely upon this escape, the physician would have to document his conclusion and would be wise to have one or more consultants' written concurrence in the record.

Informed consent procedures lend themselves to an established routine. Once adopted, this regular procedure should involve direct discussion between the patient and the physician and inclusion of a spouse or other close relative if possible. Strong efforts should be made to speak at a level of understanding suitable to the patient, and this may require using charts, pictures and even an interpreter. The discussion should be described in a timely medical record entry, and the consent form should be signed after all presentations and questions are completed. Witnessing of the patient's signature is desirable. It should never be done by a physician, however, because in court, the testimony of a physician witness in defense of a fellow doctor is not expected to sway a jury of laymen. Finally, the physician must avoid assuring a cure or successful outcome; in fact, he should clearly state that there is no guarantee of success. However, if he has reliable data available to him, he may quote the odds for successful outcome (as long as they are less than 100 percent favorable).

Who Consents for Minors?

Where the intended procedure is elective, and not urgent, and the patient is a minor or adult incompetent, consent should be obtained from a parent (who has legal custody, in case of divorce or separation) or from a court-appointed legal guardian (not just an adult with whom the child or incompetent adult is living or who is caring for him at the moment). In a true emergency, consent is implied, whether the patient is an adult, a minor, or is incompetent.

Informed Refusal

The right to informed refusal of treatment is a rather recent legally recognized concept. If, for example, a patient refuses a diagnostic test recommended by the physician, the matter should not stop there. The physician should explain what the test is intended to reveal and how the patient's health may be affected if the test information is not obtained. This explanation should be described in the patient's medical record for possible future defense of the physician.

A legally competent adult patient holds the right to refuse care, even if it leads to death. The responsibility of the attending physician is to fully disclose to the patient and his family the potentialities of nontreatment. As long as the patient is mentally competent, his decision to forgo further treatment is protected as part of the right of privacy. If a patient is competent, even though he is attached to a ventilator, he may insist upon being disconnected, and his request should be honored, provided it has been well documented that the full consequences of his decision have been explained and his competency has been established.

Special Consent

The consent for certain medical treatment or procedures must contain particular language, sometimes as required by statute. Abortion, sterilization, and implantation of investigational intraocular lenses are examples of such procedures. For terminally ill patients who do not wish to be artificially sustained when they become irreversibly comatose, a "living will" in the form established by state statute must have been executed exactly as required by law. Otherwise, doctors will be at possible risk if they refrain from life-sustaining measures.

Although childhood immunizations are routine, there are some risks of side effects of which parents may not always be aware. Consequently, the better practice is, at the least, to give to the parent, in advance of administering a vaccine, a written presentation of the risks and their incidence. The medical record should contain a notation that the information has been given to the parent.

Warning of Side Effects and Risks

The same impetus would indicate similar action when drugs are prescribed for patients. Unquestionably, it is the physician's obligation to warn the patient of significant effects of the prescribed drug and to instruct the patient to contact the physician if side effects occur. Again, a medical record notation that the warning was given would help to protect the physician against a later charge of inadequately informing the patient. If the physician regularly advises patients of the major possible side effects of prescribed drugs, that practice may influence him to alter his prescribing procedures so that the exposure of patients is limited to the least adverse potential. When the only suitable medication carries a considerable risk, not only a discussion with the patient but his signature on a properly executed consent form would be in the best interests of both physician and patient.

Perhaps the most overlooked aspect of the physician's task in obtaining informed consent is the need to emphasize the possibility of a bad result, the nature of the undesired effects, and the fallibility of the physician. To allow the patient to entrust the physician to make decisions that are the patient's responsibility is to invite anger and then thoughts of litigation when the satisfactory expectations are not fulfilled. Of course, the physician must not stress his lack of confidence in the proposed treatment to the point that he loses the patient's trust. Somehow, a proper balance of humility and confidence must be struck. Together, the patient and doctor will face their mutual uncertainties realistically if the consent process has been properly conducted. Especially to be avoided is a child-parent relationship between an adult patient and the physician. The patient should be dissuaded from projecting omnipotence upon the doctor, but not to the extent that he develops unrealistic doubt as to the physician's abilities. Rather than playing a passive role, the patient can be made a joint venturer in a medical journey, with his own duties and functions to contribute to the common cause.

Obtaining patient consent just to prevent legal risks often fails to accomplish the objective because the patient is not drawn into the reasoning and decision-making process. Without this involvement, the patient, upon discovering an unsatisfactory result of treatment, may feel betrayed, leading him to cast blame and seek revenge via a malpractice suit.

A Spokesman for Patients

The chairman of the President's Commission for the Study of Ethical Problems in Medicine and Biomedical Behavioral Research has suggested an approach to this possible communication deficit. Morris B. Abram proposes a doctor-patient relationship that facilitates sharing of information and decision-making. This would be accomplished, in part, by carrying out the legally required consent procedure whereby patients really are told about alternative treatments available and are given a full description of what is proposed to be done to them and why. To avoid the slippage made possible by the specialization of medicine, Mr. Abram calls for every hospital patient to have a physician spokesman through whom the various hospital health care teams will relate to the patient. This physician would coordinate tests, feedings, and nursing procedures—an opportunity to prevent errors—and would have the responsibility for explaining it all to the patient in an understandable way. The other physicians would not be absolved of their duty to explain what they are doing for the patient, but the designated physician would be the one who makes sure that the patient learns and understands what he needs to know in order to make reasonably intelligent choices. The patient then would be better able to carry out his task of reporting side effects and untoward reactions. With full explanations, the patient would be less surprised at, and more tolerable of, unfavorable outcomes.

By creating this kind of partnership between doctor and patient, it is hoped that defensive medicine will be reduced, many malpractice claims avoided, insurance premiums leveled, and the flight from certain high-risk specialties stopped. The cost of this innovation presumably would be covered by the savings it would bring about.

Real Cases

Let us turn now to examination of real cases, some resulting in claims, others only the subject of incident reports or insurers' investigations. Each case contains a useful lesson for those dedicated to avoiding misunderstandings that can lead to malpractice suits.

Inadequate Explanation of Proposed Procedure or Treatment

Case 1. The patient signed a consent form for plastic surgery to repair a scarred middle finger. The woman's ring finger was also deformed. The surgeon removed the ring finger, causing painful aftereffects. The patient filed suit because she had not consented to removal of the ring finger. Although there was no mention of such removal in the consent form, the surgeon insisted that it had been discussed and agreed upon. The patient had no such recollection.

This incident illustrates the maxim that unless there is an emergency or an urgent condition revealed only in the course of the surgery, no elective surgical procedure should be done if it is not covered in the written consent form.

Case 2. An orthopedic surgeon recommended a surgical procedure on the patient's foot because of a pinched nerve. He failed to advise her that the reason for doing the surgery was exploratory, to determine the cause of the pinching. Nor did he mention or suspect a cancerous condition. Later a biopsy revealed a malignant tumor and led to amputation of the leg at the knee. Suit was based upon delay in diagnosing cancer. Had the physician been candid with the patient, he would have recommended exploratory surgery and would not have lost valuable time in reaching a correct diagnosis.

Informed consent requires that the patient be told why a procedure is to be done. Not mentioning cancer in order to protect the patient from anxiety may lead to worse consequences, as occurred here. If the withholding of information is due to the patient's emotional condition, the physician should consider obtaining written consent from the patient to omit describing the procedure and the reasons for it in the usual detail. In any event, a medical record entry should be made as to why the explanation was incomplete.

Case 3. The patient was examined by an internist who, in passing, mentioned that a pigmented mole on the patient's earlobe should be seen by a specialist, since any pigmented skin lesion is suspicious. Some four months later the patient did visit a dermatologist because of a rash on his leg. The dermatologist conducted a biopsy of the mole that disclosed cancer and led to removal of part of the ear. In a suit against the internist, the patient's legal theory was failure to provide adequate information and warning so that the patient might have made an informed decision as to further care. The jury verdict found the internist 75 percent at fault and the patient 25 percent responsible for the tardiness in seeking specialty treatment.

Inasmuch as the patient was not expected to see the internist again, it was suggested that the doctor had an even greater obligation to provide the patient with all the information needed to decide whether to see a specialist about the mole.

Case 4. The patient was diagnosed as having a "false aneurysm." Two radiologists recommended treatment with percutaneous steel coil embolization. The patient consented, and the procedure was performed. Unfortunately, blood flow was cut off, and the patient's leg had to be amputated. The patient sued; she was especially distressed to learn after the fact that the surgical procedure was experimental. The consent form never mentioned the experimental nature of the treatment.

This, of course, was an indefensible case. The most basic premise of informed consent is that investigational or experimental drugs or procedures must be fully revealed to the patient, with all known risks, alternative treatments, and the expected risks of no treatment clearly disclosed.

Case 5. An ophthalmologist and patient agreed, orally, that a cryoprobe would be used to try to remedy an unsuccessful phaco-emulsification procedure on an eye having a cataract. What followed was a detached retina and loss of vision in the eye. Not only was there no written consent for the cryoprobe but there was no discussion of the risks it entailed, except that the patient was told that all surgical procedures have risks. The patient also insisted that she was told after the initial surgery that she would see again.

In this situation, the surgeon may have told the patient about the risks, but without a written consent form memorializing these warnings, he was at the mercy of the patient's memory, including the possibility that she would recall an assurance of successful surgery that occurred only in her own mind.

Case 6. A 16-year-old was referred to a physician and hospital for an abortion. She signed the usual consent form, although it was not explained to her by the physician who, in performing 30 to 40 abortions a day, relied upon referring agencies to obtain informed consent. They usually did a satisfactory job of obtaining consent, but in this out-of-state referral it was inadequately done.

There were complications following the abortion. A lawsuit was filed and then settled because, despite the fact that there was a signed and witnessed consent form, there was no proof of necessary disclosures to the patient as to the risks. The physician, even in a hurried schedule, should have assured himself that there had been informed consent, not just a signed form from the referral source.

Case 7. A bedridden arthritic needed a colonoscope procedure. Previously, she had had rectal bleeding. The technician followed the radiologist's orders and gave a cleansing enema, then a barium enema, which caused hemorrhage of the rectal vault and ultimately necessitated a colostomy.

The patient was known to have sensitive rectal tissue, so her injury was not unexpected. However, it was not mentioned in the process of obtaining consent and not noted in the consent form. A claim was made against the radiologist and the hospital where he served under contract. While it may be asking too much, the radiologist should have included in the explanation and list of risks those risks emanating from the patient's known sensitive rectal tissue.

Case 8. A patient in a dental clinic was given a consent form while reclining in the dental chair. It gave no explanation of the procedure to be performed or any of the risks. Also, it contained a statement relieving the clinic and dentist of liability if a bad result should occur.

The consent proved to be invalid, since the patient had no opportunity to read it before signing, and no description of the procedure, alternatives, and risks was given. An "exculpatory" provision, allowing escape from professional negligence, is legally unenforceable as being contrary to public policy. The clinic had intended to protect itself from the errors of its postgraduate dental students. In addition to the usual consent procedures, it should have used an educational consent form to advise the patient that he was being treated by a dentist engaged in education and training.

Failure to Reveal Risks, Side Effects, and Alternative Treatment

Case 9. After a hysterectomy, the patient's physician recommended radiation therapy in an effort to prevent recurrence of cancer. The radiation caused severe intestinal damage. The patient sued the radiologists, contending that they failed to advise her of the hazards of the therapy.

While it is not possible, nor required, to list all the possible harmful effects of a treatment, the major and more common side effects should be discussed and mentioned in the consent form.

Case 10. A pregnant patient in her late 30s was not told about the availability of amniocentesis to learn whether she was carrying a child with serious hereditary problems. The baby was born with Down's syndrome, and the parents brought a wrongful birth action. They were awarded damages for their emotional injuries brought about by being denied the opportunity for legal abortion of a defective fetus.

Whether or not the physician or parents consider abortion to be an acceptable remedy for the possibility of having a defective child, the physician should inform the expectant parents of the availability of diagnostic testing whenever there are factors that raise the possibility of an abnormal offspring. Failure to do so could expose the doctor to liability, as in this case.

Case 11. The patient signed a consent form authorizing silicone injections of the "Sakurai Formulae Procedure." Instead, the physician substituted a product labeled as "not for human use." The patient developed a nonmalignant cyst and sued the doctor. She had not been told of the substituted product.

The consent form was of no protection to the defendant doctor because the patient had not been given all the information she needed to provide a truly informed consent. Worse, the deception led to punitive damages against the physician.

Case 12. A college student had severe headaches. A neurologist referred her to a radiologist for a brain scan and arteriogram. The diagnostic tests revealed a mass near the brain. However, there were severe aftereffects of the testing, namely 45 percent bodily paralysis. The lawsuit was based on failure of the radiologist to warn the patient of side effects of the tests. The doctor said he told about a one-in-500 chance of blindness or paralysis, but the patient denied this. The case was set for trial on the issue of informed consent.

It is possible to develop prepared consent forms for the more common and risky diagnostic radiological procedures that fully cover the usual and major risks, including those that are less common but very serious. Where so recited in the consent form, there will be less of a contest of memories when the case is tried. Possibly there may be no suit at all if such a form is available for introduction into evidence.

Case 13. The physician performed a hysterectomy on a 24-year-old married woman who had two children. He had not exhausted the more conservative alternatives for treating her condition and later discovered from the pathologist's report that a healthy uterus had been removed.

The physician had not obtained a genuinely informed consent to the hysterectomy because he had not discussed the alternatives and had not given the patient the chance to choose among them.

Case 14. An obese patient underwent a jejunoileal shunt to help reduce weight. An oral explanation of the many risks included mention of jaundice. When jaundice did occur, the shunt was removed and a prolonged recovery period followed. Unfortunately, the list of risks was not in writing, so in a malpractice contest, at issue would be the doctor's memory and credibility versus the patient's.

That there was a one percent chance of liver damage and kidney problems, as well as diarrhea, if noted on the consent form, likely would have precluded suit. And if the form had dissuaded the patient from going through with the shunt procedure, there would have been far less of a loss to all concerned than what actually transpired.

Case 15. The patient had been on prescribed birth control pills for many years. She was a smoker, over 30 years of age, and in the group at greatest risk of stroke from the contraceptive pill. Her physician neither warned her of the risks nor suggested alternative medication or birth control methods.

When the patient had a stroke, causing spastic leg and arm conditions and speech loss, suit followed and a settlement was reached. Despite the routine nature of prescribing such pills, it is imperative that the physician discuss risks and alternatives and be able to prove that such a discussion took place. A timely notation in the medical record will help. Also, giving the patient a printed statement on the subject will assist in her education.

The physician should note in the record that such information was presented to the patient.

Case 16. Rushing a patient to corrective treatment may cause a short-circuiting of the consent process and expose the physician to liability for not giving the patient all the information needed to make an intelligent choice of treatments. A woman alleged that she was urged to have two moles removed from her back immediately to avoid possible malignant melanoma. Her doctor said she could not wait even one week. She did not have an opportunity for a second opinion or to explore other options. The resulting large, ugly scar after the procedure was done induced a suit that was then settled.

Even when the physician honestly believes that action should be taken quickly, unless there is a genuine emergency the patient should be told of the alternative treatments available, including what might be expected if no treatment is done or treatment is delayed. Failure to do so presents the risk that a bad result will be actionable on the theory of absence of fully informed consent.

Case 17. Where the claim appears to be one for simple malpractice, the omission of informed consent may facilitate the patient's ability to obtain compensation. A 23-year-old woman had decayed teeth. She agreed to have 10 teeth extracted and replaced with cosmetic dentures. The result was a poor fit because the dentures were anchored to decaying teeth.

In her lawsuit, the patient alleged that there had been no discussion of alternatives to extracting so many teeth. A generous settlement was reached. Even when the alternatives are clearly inferior to the recommended procedure, it is the obligation of the practitioner to present them to the patient, who is to make the ultimate decision.

Case 18. A patient consulted his physician because he was suffering from hypertension and anxiety. He was given a prescription for Eutonyl (pargyline hydrochloride) but no warning about possible adverse reactions when combined with certain foods such as cheese, chocolate, and avocados, and all forms of alcohol. The patient's adverse reactions made him unable to work for a month or two. He also claimed loss of sex drive.

The ensuing lawsuit was settled. The fact that no warning of side effects was given in this situation meant that the patient never gave informed consent to receive the medication. And if the doctor provided such a warning orally, but did not make a note of the discussion in the medical record, he made it impossible to convince a judge or jury that the full explanation had been given. However, as to loss of sex drive, such a warning could have been self-fulfilling through the power of suggestion. Here, a physician's discretion is likely to prevail as a legal defense.

Case 19. The patient was given intravenous contrast material prior to having an x-ray "scout film." An anaphylactic reaction followed, including respiratory distress, laryngeal edema, and cardiac distress. Although resuscitation was successful, the patient sued the hospital because it did not originally obtain his informed consent. There were no warnings about the side effects he experienced.

When severe reactions are known to occur, even if uncommonly, the patient should be so warned. A notation in the medical record about the warning is the least the physician should do to be able to prove that the patient really was told of the risks.

Case 20. The patient was poor, and when told of the cost of a Pap test, refused it. Eventually she died of cancer of the cervix. Her survivors were allowed to sue the doctor on the theory that he had not fully explained to the patient what harmful consequences might follow her failure to have the diagnostic test. This is the concept of informed refusal.

The doctor should so record in his charts when a patient refuses to have the test after a full explanation of its purpose and the adverse possibilities of not having the useful information the test might furnish.

Case 21. How much need a physician disclose to a patient about possible side effects of a neuroleptic drug? In this instance, tardive dyskinesia and involuntary muscle movements were the risks and did occur. The patient sued on the basis that he may well have chosen not to take the drug if the "material risks" of the particular side effects had been disclosed.

One of the issues to be tried would have been whether a hypothetical reasonable person (not the patient himself) under similar circumstances would have refused the drug if given a full description of the side effects. Of course, had these risks been disclosed, preferably in writing, there may have been no litigation over lack of informed consent.

Case 22. When is it acceptable for physicians to refrain from telling the truth about the patient's condition for "compassionate" reasons? Just to avoid sadness and disappointment is hardly adequate justification. Illustrative is a case in which a family physician referred the patient to a specialist who diagnosed multiple sclerosis in a 44-year-old woman. Neither physician told her of the diagnosis in order to protect her feelings. Not knowing of her condition, she married, quit her job, moved away, then returned and could not obtain employment. She became depressed, and a divorce followed. Upon learning of the unrevealed diagnosis, she sued both physicians for failure to disclose all material facts related to her condition and diagnosis. She lost the opportunity for some treatment and would have ordered her life differently if she had been fully informed, she claimed.

The family physician settled the suit and the neurologist was held liable for a considerable sum. Neither had any medical record notes to indicate that their nondisclosure, intended to avoid an expected emotional reaction that would have worsened the patient's condition, was justified.

Case 23. Not discussing risks of proposed therapy still is common. Radiation therapy is fraught with risks, yet the radiologist in this case never disclosed any to a patient whose intestines subsequently were damaged by the radiation.

The treatment was intended to reduce the possibility of a recurrence of cancer, but that did not excuse failure to disclose the known risks and not allowing an informed patient to determine whether to have the therapy.

Case 24. The memory gap is illustrated by the case of a patient for whom prednisone was prescribed. That there was no written consent form was not unusual. The doctor remembered telling the patient about risks of steroid therapy, but the patient recalled only that the prescription was offered "to keep him well." The side effect suffered was rather rare, but it should have been disclosed because it can result in a significant disability.

The claim was settled for a considerable amount. The legal risk might have been reduced if a printed sheet disclosing side effects of this commonly prescribed drug had been given to the patient.

Case 25. Oral warnings can help to avoid a malpractice claim even without inclusion in the consent form, provided the patient remembers what was said. When a 17-year-old boy suffered a refracture while being helped out of bed by hospital employees, his parents did not pursue a malpractice claim. The boy's physician had warned the parents of the possibility of such a refracture, so they were neither surprised nor angered when it happened.

Case 26. Radial keratotomy was an investigational procedure when an opthalmologist proposed it to the patient. However, the patient was not so advised in the consent form, nor was he told about an ongoing study as to the longterm effectiveness of the benefits of the procedure. The doctor said he mentioned these facts in conversation, but the patient claimed not to have heard them.

The unsatisfactory result of the procedure prompted a lawsuit wherein the absence of informed consent would be the key issue. Without proof of written disclosure of the investigational aspect of the procedure and of the involvement of the patient in a research study, the opthalmologist's chances of avoiding liability would be slim indeed.

Case 27. The patient and spouse, neither fluent in English, consented to a mediastinoscopy because of lymph node involvement with a tumor. Without specific consent, an extension into exploratory surgery was done and occasioned cutting the laryngeal nerve. Nurses in the operating room attempted to prevent the unauthorized surgery, but it had already commenced.

The adverse effects of the unconsented extension of surgery, not prompted by a life-threatening emergency, clearly were actionable. In this instance, perhaps because of the patient's lack of sophistication, no claim was pressed.

Case 28. The physician prescribed an IUD because the patient seemed to be anxious when taking contraceptive pills. She was told that the IUD carried no risk and only minor side effects (unless pregnant, and she was not). Pain and bleeding occurred within a few days, followed by perforation of the uterus, which required surgical repair.

In the lawsuit that followed, the court held that when a patient asks about risks, the doctor must respond truthfully. Here his response was a false representation, possibly constituting fraud. The patient was entitled to recover damages because of absence of valid consent.

Case 29. When the patient consented to a simple mastectomy, she was unaware of the alternative possibility of subcutaneous mastectomy. She would have opted for the better cosmetic potential if she had been given the choice. At least she so maintained at the trial for malpractice due to lack of informed consent. In at least one state, all the available means of treating suspected breast cancer must be explained to the patient; it is required by statute. Failure to do so could jeopardize the doctor's license as well as expose him to malpractice liability.

Case 30. All patients, including males, are entitled to full disclosure about their breast surgery. In this instance, a transsexual patient needed breasts and received silicone injections, which formed nodules. These were removed, but the patient was left with inflamed, sore, and hard areas. A subcutaneous mastectomy was performed to remedy the new problem. The patient received a large award in suing his physicians for failing to warn him of the risks of removing the original nodules.

To the extent possible, the risks of adverse results of contemplated surgery should be discussed with the patient. There can be worse consequences than his refusal to go ahead with the surgery if frightened by the recitation of risks, namely a bad result and no proof of informed consent.

Case 31. After a bad result, if a patient first learns of an alternative treatment that was not mentioned, he may insist that he would have chosen the alternative had he been aware of its availability. In this case, the bladder was inadvertently cut during a hysterectomy. In addition to suing for negligence, the patient added a claim for failure to obtain informed consent because the possibility of hormonal therapy instead of surgery had not been discussed. The court permitted the latter claim to proceed to trial.

Case 32. Genetic counseling has become a responsibility even of nonspecialists. In this case, a physician treated three generations of a family. His first patient was diagnosed as having multiple familial polyposis, a hereditary disease that often leads to cancer. Apparently, the doctor never told the patient that the condition is hereditary and should be considered before deciding to have children. Nor did the physician warn the original patient's daughter, also his patient, who grew up and had a defective child. The young mother died soon thereafter. Her widower sued the doctor for his failure to counsel any members of the family regarding their genetic risks.

In today's informational climate, when in doubt it is best to share with the patient what his medical risks may be. Even when the patient is thought to have a "dread disease," there are few occasions that legally justify nondisclosure to the patient or to close relatives who may be personally affected.

Case 33. The potential impact of certain drugs upon the fetus is information that should be impressed upon patients of child-bearing age. In this situation, the wife was given Dilantin for her epilepsy. The first child was born with a cleft palate and hirsutism. The parents assumed that these risks were the full extent of Dilantin's threat and chose to have another child. This one had growth deficiencies and was mentally and physically retarded. These possibilities were disclosed in the package insert and in *Physician's Desk Reference*, as was the risk of congenital heart disease. None of these risks were told to the couple.

The parents filed suit against the physician's employer. They stated a clear case of wrongful birth; that is, if they had been properly advised of the risks of conceiving and carrying a child while the mother is taking Dilantin, they would not have had the child. Damages in such cases may include the extraordinary costs of treating and caring for the handicapped child.

Case 34. Even mental patients have the right to refuse medication. Here, a material but not common risk of the antipsychotic drug was tardive dyskinesia. The patient was entitled to be advised of this potential side effect and to refuse the drug if so inclined. Suit was permitted because the opportunity for informed consent was denied to a patient who, although being treated for a mental condition, was not without potential understanding of these issues.

Case 35. The patient is entitled to privacy, not only of medical records but of photographs as well. When the patient gave her plastic surgeon oral permission to use "before and after" photographs to show to prospective patients, he used them in a department store promotion and on local television. Acquaintances recognized the unnamed patient. She sued the doctor and recovered substantial damages for his having gone beyond her authorization.

Obviously, it was foolhardy for the physician to use these photographs for any commercial purpose without having explicit written consent of the patient.

Case 36. Encouraging the patient to proceed with surgery when he is fearful can backfire. The patient in this litigation was told that impotence was unlikely as a result of the proposed surgical treatment for ulcerative colitis. Afterward, he was "organically impotent." The court found that the warning of the risk of impotence was not specific enough, thus allowing the suit to continue for alleged lack of informed consent.

Case 37. As long as there is a credible alternative treatment, it should be mentioned. When a child appeared for treatment of a fractured humerus, even before the x-rays were available the parents were asked to consent to surgery, which called for insertion of plates and screws. Later, ugly scars remained. When the parents learned that the alternative of immobilization was a preferred first approach to treating the fracture but was never made available to them, they sued the physician for causing a bad result without first obtaining fully informed consent.

Hindsight facilitates listing of alternatives that should have been discussed, but even a quick run-through of alternatives and why they are less suitable under the circumstances can help to guard against this kind of lawsuit.

Case 38. Similarly, a woman whose ovaries and reproductive organs were removed later discovered that she could have been treated without submitting to surgery. She contended that the surgical removal of her organs was unnecessary and done in absence of fully informed consent. She sued the surgeon.

Again, it would not have taken long to discuss the nonsurgical alternatives, which perhaps would have been rejected by the patient. Without such disclosure, the surgeon was exposed to application of retrospective wisdom on the part of the dissatisfied patient.

Case 39. When a patient was discharged from a hospital, he was given Prolixin and Thorazine but without warnings as to their effects. He drank alcohol, drove a car, and hit a tree, severely injuring his passenger. Suit was filed against the physicians and the hospital for not warning the patient to avoid drinking and/or driving while taking the medications. The court held that what happened to him was a reasonably foreseeable result of failure to warn the patient of known risks. Had there been a warning, of course, it would have to have been noted in the medical record to be provable.

Case 40. To illustrate the "damned if you do and damned if you don't" situation, consider this one. The patient was told that pathological tests had indicated cancer, and surgery was recommended. She had the surgery and no cancer was found. The patient then learned that the particular pathology test had a 10 percent chance of error and that the falsely indicated cancer was of a slow-growing variety. Therefore, she should have been counseled to delay the surgery for a reasonable time while the tests were repeated.

The patient sued the surgeon for unduly rushing to operate instead of waiting and retesting. The case was settled. A realistic assessment of the urgency of surgery—to the patient—is one of the obligations in the process of obtaining informed consent.

Honesty in Discussing Unfavorable Outcome

Case 41. After abdominal surgery, the patient developed adhesions. He was unhappy about the need for further surgery to correct them, especially when he no longer had health insurance protection. His physician carefully and considerately explained that adhesions are not uncommon in this situation without the occurrence of malpractice. The patient ultimately accepted the doctor's explanation and refrained from filing the suit he had threatened.

Case 42. In contrast is this case. The patient had a breast removed. Subsequently, the pathologist changed his reading so that it was not a malignant situation after all and removal of the breast proved not to have been necessary. The surgeon failed to tell the patient about the "error" for six months. Upon learning the truth, the angered patient sued him.

One cannot be certain, but it is likely that the patient's impetus to sue the surgeon might have been reduced if a timely admission of the changed pathological diagnosis had been conveyed to her.

Case 43. An unemployed, aging male actor had plastic surgery on his face. An undesired result was a bald spot in the temporal area, anticipated, however, in obtaining consent. Having expected perfection, the patient sued despite the surgeon's expressed concern and offer to pay for a hairpiece.

For some patients, unrealistic expectations cannot be overcome even by a physician's considerate care, attentiveness, and prompt divulgence of any untoward developments. Judging the patient's anticipation of a particular result—and addressing it prior to surgery—may be a useful approach to the problem.

Case 44. That honesty is usually the best policy is illustrated by this case of a broken needle. It was part of a suture needle left in the patient's abdomen. When it was later discovered, surgical removal was successfully accomplished, but the angered patient filed suit. The surgeon originally had decided to leave the needle fragment in the patient, hoping it would cause no harm and would not be discovered. He took a chance and was caught.

Had the surgeon advised the patient about the portion of needle left in the abdominal region and arranged for prompt removal, the risk of suit would have been much reduced.

Case 45. The patient died due to an embolism when air entered the aortic line during open heart surgery. The widow was told that the death was "just one of those things." About two years later she learned, through the office of the chief medical examiner of the state, the true cause of death. She then sued the hospital and the supplier of the medical equipment. The statute of limitations did not bar suit because she did not discover the possibility of malpractice—due to lack of truthfulness—until a couple of years after the patient's death.

Case 46. The patient had been in the labor room for many hours before being taken to the delivery room. The obstetrician came to the waiting room and told the expectant first-time father, "We've had seven hours of unproductive labor. We're going to have to terminate the pregnancy."

The father, frightened and perplexed by the terminology, replied, "Terminate! Does that mean someone has to die?"

"No, of course not," the doctor responded with evident irritation, "we're going to do a section."

The results were uneventful and no one died. However, considering the physician's inability to communicate intelligibly with laymen, it was not surprising that he was successfully sued by subsequently dissatisfied patients.

Conveying Overconfidence or Assuring Successful Outcome

Case 47. A physician assured his patient that there would be no visible scarring if dermatofibromas were removed using liquid nitrogen. There were such scars and the patient sued.

There is no need to make unrealistic assurances. These may be held to be, in law, a guarantee of a successful result. Then, failure to achieve complete success is a breach of contract and compensable even if no negligence was committed by the physician. Instilling confidence should be possible without offering a guarantee of a cure.

Case 48. The physician had difficulty in performing amniocentesis. Three attempts produced fluid with blood in it, and it could not be evaluated. The patient was told the fetus was normal despite failure to detect fetal heartbeat. In fact, the fetus was dead and the subsequent stillbirth and inquiry indicated that a possible cause of death was the amniocentesis procedure. The parents sued the physician.

The doctor bungled the amniocentesis, knew it, refused to admit it, and compounded the error by assuring the patient without having any basis for doing so. He had no defense to the malpractice suit, and the parents had no reason to be sympathetic toward him in their effort to maximize the damage award.

Case 49. The patient became pregnant after undergoing sterilization. She then discovered that the doctor had assured her that the proper amount of fallopian tube had been removed when he knew that less had been taken out. This was fraudulent concealment, which permitted bringing suit after the statute of limitation otherwise would have barred it. Reassuring the patient in this case was more than overconfidence; it was deception, an unacceptable component of the doctor-patient relationship.

Performing a Procedure Not Consented to By the Patient

Case 50. A Medicaid patient consented to the repair of an enterocele and rectocele. However, the physician went on to do a revision of the vagina and reconstruction of perineal body. This was surgery incidental to the intended procedure, but it was not consented to by the patient. Later she encountered such pain in attempting sex that she was unable to have it.

The patient brought suit. A defense would have been difficult, since the unconsented surgery was not required by any emergency.

Case 51. The patient agreed to surgical repair of a hiatal hernia. In addition, a vagotomy and pyloroplasty were done, although these procedures were not absolutely necessary. The additional surgery caused tearing of gastric vessels and led to a splenectomy. A suit was filed because of the unauthorized procedures. Had they been anticipated, discussed with and approved by the patient, the added procedures and bad results may have been defensible, since the loss of the spleen may not have harmed the patient's health.

Case 52. In a most unfortunate extension of authorized surgery, the surgeon performed an agreed-upon laparoscopy but then added a hysterectomy and bilateral oophorectomy. The additional surgery resulted in brain damage.

Obviously, unconsented removal of organs should be avoided. When those are reproductive organs, the risk of liability is greater, even in absence of negligence in the performance of the extra procedure and no complications.

Case 53. There is a defense to the claim for damages when inadequate explanation of the scope of surgery is given. The argument is that a hypothetical reasonable patient would have accepted the extended surgery if told the full story. Therefore, the real patient was no worse off for having received incomplete information. This occurred in a case where the patient consented to a cystoscopy with dilation, but got a urethrotomy with subsequent incontinence.

Although the doctor did not lose the malpractice suit, had he gone on to discuss the urethrotomy with the patient, he likely would have been saved the agony of the litigation.

Case 54. An overweight 23-year-old woman with no children had had much abdominal surgery, was an overuser of painkillers, and begged the physician to do a laparotomy. In the process he removed the uterus, which turned out not to be diseased. There was no written form covering the hysterectomy or the sterilization effect. The patient was a licensed vocational nurse and probably knew that removal of the uterus would mean sterilization. Nevertheless, she sued.

Irrespective of the patient's technical knowledge, it is essential to obtain a written consent to any procedure that will render her unable to conceive. This case also teaches that the physician should not allow the patient to persuade him to do a procedure he thinks is unwarranted.

Case 55. Providing psychiatric care to a child requires prior consent of the custodial parent. In this case, the mother, who was not the custodial parent, brought the child to a psychiatrist for a year without the father's consent. The father sued the psychiatrist upon learning of what happened. Although the child may not have been harmed, his treatment was not consented to by the custodial parent and some damages might have been awarded anyway for infliction of emotional damages on the father.

Case 56. Is it legal or ethical to perform a surgical procedure on a cancer patient, which would be useless under the circumstances, in order to avoid revealing to the patient that she has cancer? This was the issue when, on the day a laminectomy was scheduled, the surgeon advised the patient's husband for the first time that she had cancer. The husband felt that the patient could not handle news of cancer, so authorized proceeding with the pointless laminectomy. The patient had the surgery and eventually died of cancer.

The surgeon and attending physicians were sued, accused of withholding the cancer news from the patient so they might earn the fees from the laminectomy. Since the patient herself was not known to be mentally incompetent, it was deceptive to have operated on her without disclosing that the procedure would have no lasting benefit because of the cancer. If the physicians preferred not to upset the patient with the announcement about the cancer, they should, nevertheless have found a way to postpone the laminectomy.

Case 57. Bad results often lead to liability under questionable circumstances. In this case, the pregnant patient was a candidate for a cesarean section. However, the hospital's rules required a second opinion before doing a first-time c-section. The doctor contacted for the second opinion thought that labor had begun spontaneously and ordered injection of Pitocin to further induce labor, despite the patient's objection. When the attending physician arrived, he was displeased at hearing of the injection. The birth was difficult, and a brain damaged baby emerged.

The mother sued the consultant who had insisted on the injection of Pitocin—considered unauthorized treatment because the patient had objected to it—and the court recognized this as a case of unconsented treatment. It was, of course, a failure of communication between two physicians with the confused patient caught in the middle, all of which made her lawsuit easier to prove.

Case 58. In the absence of a real emergency, a competent adult patient must be the one to consent to surgical extensions, and not even a spouse can give binding consent to additional surgery. Here the patient signed a consent form for a laparoscopy. During surgery, the physician found adhesions that prevented his doing the intended procedure and decided to perform a salpingectomy instead. He then deemed a total abdominal hysterectomy appropriate and obtained the husband's consent. Unfortunately, the patient suffered brain damage as a consequence of the surgery. Her guardian sued the physician, contending that the patient's own consent to the hysterectomy was required but not obtained.

Permission for a procedure that renders the patient unable to have children should be given by her and not only by her husband (unless she is legally incompetent and he is her legal guardian or she is temporarily incompetent and the procedure is necessary to save her life).

Case 59. A mother brought her child to a dentist for two teeth to be filled. In fact, eight teeth were filled. The child's nausea in reaction to nitrous oxide added to the discontent and stimulated a malpractice suit. The dentist insisted that it was customary to fill all teeth needing treatment as indicated by a clinical examination. He won despite his casual attitude that brought on the suit. Better practice would have been to obtain specific consent to all nonemergency care.

Failure to Document or to Make Timely Entries

Proper recording of what was said between patient or physician, or between physicians, or between physician and allied health personnel, or what was done, and making record entries soon after the events transpired often makes the difference in whether a suit is filed or not. And it may determine whether a suit can be effectively defended.

Case 60. The patient was involved in a theatrical production, so he asked the physician to set his broken radius in a half-shell cast. The doctor reluctantly agreed, but made no record entry of the reason for the limited cast. Later he switched to a short arm plaster cast. The result was unsatisfactory; another operation was needed, and a long arm fibrous glass cast was fitted. Some arm motion was lost permanently.

Suit was filed. The doctor's defense was hampered by absence of any notation about acceding to the patient's original request for less than optimal treatment.

Case 61. The patient claimed that his physician authorized him to make a business trip and that this caused aggravation of the patient's foot problem. The doctor said he expressly forbade the trip, but that the patient refused to listen. Failure of the doctor to record this aspect of the conversation prevented a quick end to the dispute.

Case 62. Careless consent practice was illustrated by this lawsuit. The patient signed a consent to plastic surgery while in the hospital, but it did not reflect any prior discussion in the doctor's office. In fact, the doctor obtained no consent form in his office and made no notations as to the discussion with the patient. Since the patient was unhappy with the results, he was in position to claim that his consent was not informed and thus was not effective.

Case 63. After a bad result following a cataract procedure, and upon learning of a possible malpractice claim, the doctor made retrospective entries in the hospital record that appeared to have been made before the surgery. He wrote that he had described the risks to the patient before obtaining consent. Unfortunately for the physician, the patient's attorney had obtained a copy of the medical records as they existed before the added entry.

This error in judgment was potentially disastrous because the medical procedure was done properly, not negligently, and the physician really had made the explanation to the patient; he simply had failed to note it in a timely way. The late entry, appearing to be deceptive, meant that the patient would surely obtain some compensation from a jury even if undeserved.

Case 64. The physician, who had a casual attitude toward record keeping, failed to make notes on each visit by the patient and of medications given directly to him. When an unsatisfactory result occurred, the patient sued. Settlement was compelled by the haphazard records of the doctor. If he had been subjected to cross-examination at the trial, he would have made a poor impression on the jury.

Case 65. In this case, the deceased patient had refused certain tests and treatment, probably for financial reasons. In the medical record there appeared an out-of-place entry to the effect that the patient had refused further examinations and repeat studies. At issue was the timing of these entries; they were possibly self-serving for protection of the physician.

An otherwise defensible malpractice case was prolonged because the apparently late entries raised questions about the physician's credibility.

Case 66. The patient refused hospitalization for anxiety and depression. After she left the doctor's office, she had an automobile accident. The police accused her of being drunk, but she was actually affected by Inderal, Librium, and possibly other mood-altering drugs. The patient then sued the doctor for not warning her to refrain from driving while taking these drugs. (She should have been aware of the risk, since she had been in a previous accident.)

Standard practice should have been to make a note in the medical record of the oral warning to the patient about driving or operating machinery while taking the particular drugs. Additionally, the prescriptions should have directed the pharmacist to place a warning sticker on the container. Had the doctor done so, a judge or jury would have been more inclined to believe the prescriber than the patient.

Case 67. The patient was referred to a radiologist who had problems with positioning the patient and could not complete the x-ray series. He failed to notify the referring physician that not all the requested x-rays had been taken. Upon reading the radiologist's report, the generalist reasonably assumed there were no spinal fractures. Unfortunately, the missing x-rays were to have covered that area.

The radiologist was exposed to liability for failing to inform the referring physician of the incomplete scope of the x-ray series.

Case 68. The patient was diagnosed as having breast cancer. Although chemotherapy was recommended, she refused it. The physician failed to note the refusal in the medical records. Much later, the patient decided to accept chemotherapy. Her treating physician said that it was too late to be useful, since chemotherapy should have followed soon after breast surgery.

The patient then found a physician who would try belated chemotherapy. Nevertheless, the patient sued the first doctor for the delay. A simple notation in that doctor's records about the patient's initial refusal might have precluded the litigation.

Case 69. Before performing a tubal ligation, the physician had the patient and her spouse sign consent forms that included the statement that sterilization procedures sometimes prove ineffective even though no medical negligence has occurred. This greatly helped in the defense of the claim for malpractice because of an ineffective tubal ligation. Emphasis of this point during the discussion prior to signing of the consent forms would have assisted, and a timely notation about the presentation in the medical records also would have benefited the physician.

Case 70. Even winning a malpractice suit can be a partial loss. Litigation is upsetting to the defendant practitioner, and it can cause his malpractice insurance premiums to increase. In this case, the orthopedic surgeon obtained the patient's oral consent to foot surgery after explaining the possibility of nonunion. After a bad result of the surgery, the patient sued, denying having given informed consent. The court found that oral consent is effective, if proved. Furthermore, in this instance, even if the consent was imcomplete, the court felt that the patient would have undergone the surgery irrespective of the adequacy of the explanations given by the physician.

If a proper written consent had been obtained, there likely would have been no suit.

Case 71. Similarly, the physician in this case obtained oral consent to perform a sterilization procedure. The patient said there was no warning that some sterilization procedures are ineffective. The failure of the sterilization led to the suit. The court held that no prudent person would have forgone the procedure upon learning that a tiny percentage of such operations are unsuccessful.

Had there been a written consent form containing the usual warnings, litigation surely would have been discouraged.

Case 72. The patient was a disabled schizophrenic veteran. The urologist was not aware of his mental problems and obtained the patient's consent to remove a testicle. In fact, the patient was not mentally competent, and his wife had been handling his affairs. The Veterans Administration had been treating her as if legal guardian even though she never received a court appointment. After a bad result, the hospital was sued and found not to have obtained informed consent because the wife was not involved. Damages were awarded.

Although the physician may not have had enough contact with the patient to suspect his mental disability, a written consent for removal of a testicle might well have included signature of the spouse, if available. Removal of genitalia routinely should be consented to also by the spouse, if possible, even though it is not absolutely essential when the patient is a mentally competent adult.

Case 73. Communication failure between an oncologist and referring physician ended in a suit against both. The physician diagnosed rectal cancer and referred the patient to the radiation oncologist to shrink the tumor prior to surgery. After radiation therapy, the oncologist advised the physician to wait four to six weeks before surgery. This was done in writing, but the physician claimed not to have received the information and delayed surgery by only two weeks. Postoperative incontinence led to a suit against the two doctors. Because the oncologist could show that his comments were written, the jury believed him and held against the referring physician alone.

Case 74. When a medical record entry is falsified, there is a risk of an award of punitive damages in addition to compensatory damages. That could have happened in this case, except that the jury found no negligence in the care of the elderly patient by the hospital, and by practitioners who treated her, irrespective of any falsified entries. There can be no punitive damages in absence of an award of basic compensatory damages.

Following progress notes in the medical records, there appeared a predated note professing to be postsurgical, saying that all went well as of that time. The physician was unable to explain why a favorable report was entered late and predated. Since the patient actually had a poor result, this entry raised suspicion of a retroactive attempt to exclude questions about operating room negligence, and place blame on postoperative care. A suit was filed.

Communicating with Non-English Speaking Patients

Consent cannot be obtained unless there is a reasonable understanding by the patient (or parent or legal guardian) of the diagnosis, prognosis, proposed treatment, risks, alternatives, and expectations if the patient should opt for no treatment. When the patient and physician do not speak or understand a common tongue, an interpreter may be required. Consent forms in languages other than English are available and should be used if suitable.

Case 75. The patient suffered a smashed finger in an industrial accident. He spoke only Spanish and was treated by two physicians and a nurse, all familiar with Spanish. An interpreter also was involved. The patient first agreed to amputation, then said, "no." Later he accepted amputation and signed the English consent form agreeing to it. Medical records contained notes as to this consent.

When a bad result occurred, the patient contended that he never really consented to amputation. Although the consent form was in English, a language he did not understand, the witnesses and medical record entries provided adequate protection against the lawsuit.

Case 76. This case covers a rather sensitive area. The Spanish-speaking patient agreed to a cesarean section and tubal ligation, an interpreter having explained the end result of sterilization procedures. The consent form, in Spanish, was signed by the patient. However, it failed to specifically cover sterilization. A separate form intended for that purpose was forgotten. After the procedures were completed, the patient had a change of mind and decided she hadn't wanted to be sterilized after all.

One way to protect against such a change of heart, after it is too late, is to have the patient write on the consent form in her own language that she understands that the procedure she has consented to will render her incapable of having children. Then, when confronted by her unknowing husband (whose consent is not essential), she will not be able to blame the hospital and physicians for allegedly tricking her into an unanticipated sterilization procedure.

Case 77. Using as interpreter a person who is not fully conversant in the foreign language is a risky practice, although the interpreter does the best he can. In this case, the patient was having a difficult delivery. The doctor was communicating with her through a delivery room attendant serving as interpreter. Apparently, some of the doctor's instructions to the patient were poorly or incorrectly interpreted. The baby died, and the doctor was sued for negligence in prenatal care and in the delivery. The translation problem contributed to the risk of liability being found in this case.

Failure to Warn Victim of Death Threats by Patient

Case 78. A psychiatrist was told by his patient that he intended to physically harm or kill his live-in girlfriend. Guarding the psychotherapist-patient confidential relationship, the therapist revealed to no one what the patient intended, although he believed the patient to be capable of carrying out his criminal intention. The patient not only killed his girlfriend, but her child saw the murder and was emotionally damaged. The boy successfully sued the therapist for his own anxieties and for the death of his mother.

The psychotherapist practiced in a state where the law has been interpreted by the courts to require practitioners to warn the intended victim of violence, or the local police, so that protective measures may be taken against the disturbed patient. The therapist-patient confidentiality is superseded by the therapist's obligation to the public and to public safety. Although threats of suicide need not be reported, when an identifiable prospective victim is threatened with physical harm, the therapist must take action to warn the victim, or local police, or else be exposed to liability for the consequences. This is so even though a psychiatrist cannot be certain whether his patient really will do violence, or if he is merely ventilating or hallucinating. It is a choice between protecting the therapist from legal liability or risking loss of patient confidence and candor. Since this book is about avoiding malpractice, the preferred option is to report on the patient rather than to maintain silent confidentiality.

CHAPTER FOUR

Diagnostic and Treatment Failures

FAILURE to diagnose has become a leading cause given for bringing malpractice actions. An increasingly troublesome area has been that of delayed diagnosis, especially of cancer. There is a public perception—perhaps stimulated by statements that cancer is curable if acted upon quickly—that most cancers can be cured or arrested if a timely diagnosis is made.

It is more appropriate for physicians, not lawyers, to advise on how to improve medical practices and professional skills so as to improve diagnostic success and assure proper care of patients. Nevertheless, the lawsuits and malpractice claims examined for purposes of this book provide ample illustrations of what to do and what to eschew, oftentimes describing incidents not readily available in medical publications.

Undertaking Cases Beyond the Practitioner's Ability

Case 79. An overweight 30-year-old male patient sought surgery to remedy his obesity. The physician, without exhausting medical approaches to weight reduction, performed the surgery. It was a procedure he had never tried before, nor had he seen it done. The patient's stomach was perforated and he died.

Suit was brought against the hospital for its failure to police the physician and allowing him to conduct a surgical procedure without going through the credentialing process to prove his qualifications to perform it. The physician, of course, had no defense, having turned the patient into an experimental subject without his knowledge. Both defendants wisely settled rather than face the potential ire of a jury.

Case 80. Although not formally trained in plastic surgery, a physician performed such a procedure on a woman who had had previous plastic surgery elsewhere. Her emotional status was questionable, and when the procedure produced swelling and infection, she stopped payment on her check and threatened suit. The physician probably should have arranged for a psychiatric consultation on the patient before operating. However, his lack of formal training in plastic surgery left him vulnerable to liability any time his patient had a bad result, even without provable malpractice. He should have refrained from practicing plastic surgery, especially on a disturbed person.

Case 81. A general surgeon did a "tummy tuck," but did not employ plastic surgery techniques. The patient was left with folds of skin on the hips and an unattractive scar above the bikini line that had a rough, irritating edge. Allegedly, the surgeon had promised a much lower scar. The jury awarded both compensatory and punitive damages against the surgeon, by then retired from practice. It was a high price to pay for a procedure that a general surgeon should not have undertaken because he could not be confident of accomplishing the desired result.

Case 82. During surgery for a dental implant, possibly too much force was used. Three teeth were loosened, necessitating root canal work. The physician recognized that he had erred. When the patient first suggested that he would be content with having the dental work paid for, the physician quickly accepted the settlement offer. It was a wise decision. The physician learned (1) that his technique was defective, and (2) he demonstrated that concern for the patient after a bad result can be the least damaging to the pocketbook and the doctor-patient relationship.

Case 83. An incorrect diagnosis of the patient's eye problem led to treatment that caused photocoagulation. It turned out that the patient's original condition would have cleared up without treatment. By undergoing inappropriate treatment, he suffered severe loss of vision. Perhaps engaging a consultant would have saved both the patient's eyesight and the physician from a malpractice claim that he would not very well defend.

Case 84. A 38-year-old patient with Peyronie's disease had curvature of the penis and diminished sexual function. Conservative treatment was ineffective, so surgery was attempted. Part of the penis was removed to eliminate hardened tissue, but too much erectile tissue was taken. The patient suffered emotionally, too, and sued the surgeon. The award was $750,000 to him and $250,000 to his wife for her loss of consortium.

Any procedure that may worsen sexual function should be done only by those extremely well versed in the technique. Bad results in such cases can be very costly because of juries' sympathy for the patient and spouse.

Case 85. Prescribing drugs in dosages well in excess of the manufacturer's recommendations presents potential for nondefensible claims. Here the doctor began the diabetic patient on an oral hypoglycemic agent at 1,000 mg per day. The package insert had suggested 250 mg per day, a small initial dosage, and never more than 750 mg a day. The patient experienced fever, rash, and soreness before the prescriber's partner intervened and stopped all medications. Eventually the patient worsened, had surgery, and died. In the lawsuit that followed, it was contended that the misprescribing set in motion the sad train of events.

An approved drug may be prescribed by a physician for whatever reasons and in such dosage as he chooses. However, exceeding the manufacturer's recommendations places the prescriber at legal risk when there are untoward results. The suggested usage and dosage of most drugs are readily available in *Physicians' Desk Reference,* so there is little excuse available in court for not being familiar with them.

Case 86. A family practitioner chose cryosurgery for treating the patient's internal hemorrhoids. Despite her training in this procedure, there was a bad result. The patient sued and produced as an expert witness a specialist from another specialty. His testimony was permitted, thus measuring the family practitioner against a standard of another, more specialized branch of medicine. A verdict for the patient was not unexpected. When it comes to a particular procedure, the generalist risks being judged according to a single national standard created by specialists who customarily perform the procedure.

Case 87. When it can be shown that a physician should have known better, he is vulnerable to malpractice liability. Consider the doctor who treated a young laborer's fractured elbow with a prosthesis known as a Coonrad device. It failed, and the second procedure was less than optimal in result. The patient sued, contending that a Coonrad device was inappropriate for a man who needed strength in his elbow. Furthermore, its success rate was too low to be acceptable under the circumstances.

Case 88. Semiexperimental treatment, or doing something different just because prior procedures haven't helped the patient, invites liability for further unsatisfactory results. In this case, because previous treatment had not succeeded, the physician tried manipulation of the shoulder while the patient, an architect, was unconscious under anesthesia. After the second such treatment, the patient awoke with his arm overhead and painful; in fact, the shoulder was dislocated. Remedial care left him with lack of complete arm motion and full use of his hand, a serious matter for an architect. A substantial award was made in his lawsuit.

Failure to Be Thorough in Examination or in Ordering Tests

Contemporary practitioners are torn between entreaties to avoid unnecessary, expensive examinations and tests and the fear of malpractice liability if they fail to examine or test and thus miss a diagnosis altogether or delay the correct diagnosis. If the objective is to escape from the threat of malpractice suits, the practitioner will choose to be overcautious even if not economical. The patient or third-party payer may have to pay handsomely for this attempt at error-free care, but the cases described below indicate the wisdom of being thorough in examination and testing.

Case 89. To a layman, it would seem that a patient with a chronic knee problem should be x-rayed at some point in the treatment process. Therefore, the physician-defendant in this case was in a difficult position to defend himself. He was board certified in orthopedics. After making an incorrect diagnosis, he finally referred the patient for arthroscopy, at which time he was x-rayed for the first time. The x-ray revealed a giant-cell tumor, excision of which necessitated removal of the knee and substitution of a prosthetic implant. The jury was instructed as to the patient's loss of a chance at saving his knee because the x-ray was not done at the earlier time.

The physician would have needed an excellent professional reason for not ordering the x-ray when it could have been especially helpful. Even if the patient might not have fared much better with an earlier correct diagnosis through a timely x-ray, juries tend to be generous to those with a bad result whose correct diagnosis was delayed because of inadequate testing and who therefore suffered the agonies of not knowing the cause of their problems.

Case 90. The patient was treated by the same ophthalmologist from age 23 to 32. No tonometer testing was done, since such tests were customarily reserved for patients over 40 who would be in the age group at risk for glaucoma. The patient did have glaucoma and successfully sued the physician. Although his practice was consistent with that of his specialty in not doing routine tonometry in patients under 40, the court would not let him hide behind a professional standard or custom when a cheap, simple, and usually harmless test might have made possible a timely diagnosis.

Case 91. A mother agreed to be donor of a kidney for her daughter. The mother had a discoloration on one breast, so a mammogram was ordered. Unfortunately, the test was not carried out. After the kidney was transplanted, the mother was diagnosed as having breast cancer. Did she donate a cancerous kidney to her child? The answer would not be known for a long time. Mother and daughter sued, and the defendants wisely settled.

Here the proper test was ordered, but poor communications and followup permitted the transplant to take place without the test results. So it is not enough to order tests; the results must be obtained and evaluated before elective treatment proceeds. Otherwise, the providers are vulnerable to liability if that test might have precluded erroneous action.

Case 92. An emergency room patient had been struck in the head by a sword. He may have been inebriated and was somewhat confused, but he was not aware of having been unconscious at any time. No skull x-rays were taken. The patient awoke at home with intense headache, but his mother was told by a hospital attendant that headache after such an injury is to be expected. Ice packs were recommended. Soon thereafter, the patient could not be awakened, and he subsequently died. A settlement was reached with the hospital defendant.

Absence of a skull x-ray, plus the casual advice of the hospital employee in response to a serious symptom, made a defense most difficult. Had the x-ray been taken, the gravity of the injury might have been detected. A jury would likely have thought so.

Case 93. A general practitioner who misses a diagnosis and does not refer the patient to specialists quickly enough may find that the specialists who do get the patient, but too late, will turn on the generalist. That is what happened when the patient received only a superficial examination after complaining of a swollen, inflamed abdomen. In five more visits, nothing was determined. By the time the patient reached more competent physicians, she was found to have a malignant ovarian cyst that had spread. She died.

The expected lawsuit was settled when defense counsel contacted consulting specialists, all of whom condemned the generalist's poor diagnostic practices. Had the generalist acted with greater care, the patient might have been diagnosed much earlier and the doctor would have found that the cancer had already spread. Because he did not do a thorough and timely examination, however, the generalist was at risk of being held to have deprived the patient of a chance at a cure or life prolonging treatment.

Case 94. The "lost chance" theory is indeed a growing risk, especially in cancer cases. Consider this instance. The physician did a breast biopsy, which showed a precancerous condition. On subsequent visits, the patient complained of feeling lumps, but not until she saw another physician was metastatic carcinoma diagnosed. The patient died. Her widower sued the first doctor, whose defense was that even if he had diagnosed the patient properly she still would have succumbed to breast cancer.

The widower's case was predicated on a showing that early diagnosis would have given the patient a 65 percent chance of survival, whereas the late diagnosis reduced her chances to only 20 percent. This is a thesis that convinces juries, and they are allowed to act on it. Understandably, the suit was settled rather than tried.

Case 95. Timely ordering of tests and acting on the results is not a complete defense to malpractice charges. The tests must be done properly and, if possible, adverse indications should be double-checked by whatever means are available. A patient who had "burning" in the chest and difficulty in swallowing submitted to biopsies. Cancer was indicated and parts of the esophagus and stomach were removed. Subsequently, it was found that there had been no cancer. The patient suffered terribly from the aftereffects of the surgery. He sued and won a massive award.

Case 96. Thoroughness of testing was at issue in a case arising in a hospital emergency room. An auto accident victim was found to have a jaw injury. He was discharged on a stretcher, in the care of friends, to be brought to an oral surgeon for needed treatment. Because no x-rays were taken of the rest of the body, it was not discovered that the patient had also suffered a fractured pelvis. This failure to do enough diagnostic testing exposed the hospital to malpractice liability for the consequences of the delay in obtaining diagnosis and in obtaining proper treatment.

Case 97. One would expect that full documentation of a complete workup would be done prior to a laminectomy. Here the workup was incomplete and the recording was rather casual. Furthermore, the medical records did not include all the patient's complaints about his physical condition. After poor results from the laminectomy, he denied making complaints that, if properly recorded, would have justified the operation.

Where there is an unfavorable result of a procedure, weakness in the ordering of tests, in conducting the examination, and in justifying the treatment may be revealed by the medical records, especially by absence of notations.

Sometimes the problem is one of *proving* thoroughness rather than one of not having been thorough. The test or examination may not be provable if it is not recorded.

Case 98. Doing a complete examination and responding to it in an honest manner are required by professional standards and professional ethics. Waiving either one, even at the request of a troubled patient, can lead to liability. A physician learned this when a 64-year-old patient claimed that he was disabled due to emphysema and other problems. The doctor cooperated, concluding that the patient was indeed disabled. Unanticipated by the patient were these events: He lost his job and the possibility of a pension and he did not qualify for the Social Security disability payment program. The patient then went to a large medical center, where he was found not to be disabled after all.

In an illustration of the meaning of "chutzpah," (Yiddish for extreme gall or nerve), the patient sued the doctor for causing all of his difficulties by declaring him to be disabled in the first place. The doctor, guilty of being too amenable, settled by making a modest cash payment.

Case 99. The importance of early testing and diagnosis in cancer cases was demonstrated by this case. The physician diagnosed proctitis and colitis, but did not order sigmoidoscopic examination and barium x-rays of the lower gastrointestinal tract. Had he done so, the patient's adenocarcinoma might have been diagnosed seven months earlier, increasing his chances of survival (5 years) from 15 percent to between 50 percent and 80 percent. This is not the kind of case to present before a jury.

Case 100. How extreme can this "lost opportunity" for a chance of survival get? Consider these circumstances: A timely x-ray showed a lung lesion of 4 cm. No action was taken. A year later, x-rays revealed an increase in size of the lesion. Ultimately, a tumor was removed, but after a stormy course the patient died. It was shown that the patient's chances of survival if operated on in response to the first x-ray were only 40 percent. By the time surgery occurred, the favorable possibilities were reduced to 15 percent. This reduction in chances of survival was something the jury should be permitted to consider, the court held.

Thus, even though the doctor did not cause the cancer, and even if he had acted promptly his patient had a less than 50/50 chance of survival, the doctor could be liable in damages because his delay reduced the patient's odds of surviving even more. Because early diagnosis and treatment of cancer has become the standard, deviations can be costly even if the patient's odds were never very good.

Case 101. If asked to provide professional information and guidance, a physician has an obligation to do a thorough job of testing and counseling. Here the patient feared that if she had children they might be hemophiliacs, since two of her cousins were so afflicted. She contacted two physicians, who were to do necessary tests and also check whether the cousins were registered hemophiliacs. Further, they were to examine a deceased cousin's death certificate. The doctors' conclusion was that the risk of the patient's giving birth to a hemophiliac was "very low." Consequently, the woman proceeded to have a child. It was a hemophiliac.

It seemed that there was no reliable test for Factor IX hemophilia, but the mother was not so informed. Had she been notified of this lack of assurance, she alleged that she would not have conceived or would have aborted the baby she carried. Both the parents and the child were permitted to bring a lawsuit against the parties who did an incomplete job of investigating and counseling.

Case 102. When a patient asks for an x-ray to rule out a fracture, it pays to accede to his request if not otherwise contraindicated. Example: A 15-year-old boy with a two-year history of elbow pain came to a hospital emergency room. The physician told the father that an x-ray was not necessary. In fact, as was discovered nine months later, an old fracture extended into a joint surface. Although immobilization at the time the father requested the x-ray would not have affected the result, refusal to take the x-ray prompted the later suit and financial settlement.

Case 103. Even emotionally disturbed patients have physical ailments. Therefore, it is risky to skimp on diagnostic testing because psychosomatic causation seems evident. Consider the case of such a patient whose bleeding and bowel habit changes were attributed by the physician to hemorrhoids and emotional problems. In fact, the patient had rectal cancer. Delay in doing a proctosigmoidoscopy or simple anoscopy delayed diagnosis seven weeks, placing the physician at risk of malpractice liability.

Case 104. After the patient had a stillbirth, review of the prior events revealed that she had come to the hospital twice on the day of delivery. The attending physician failed to search for fetal heartbeat on the second visit, did not diagnose pregnancy-induced hypertension, did not induce labor, did not do repeat stress tests to assess fetal condition, allowed pregnancy to go beyond term, did not obtain a consultation on a high-risk pregnancy, did not do a cesarean section, and did not use a fetal monitor when labor began. The omission of testing and monitoring in this case was overwhelming, and the legal liability potential was at the maximum.

Case 105. When a barium x-ray indicated a polyp in the colon, the physician decided to do a colonoscopy. Twice he had to abort it because of "muddy water." A perforated colon led to infection and death. The trial featured medical witnesses who testified that a colonoscopy should be started only after verifying that the bowel is free of feces and other obstruction to visibility. The doctor was held liable because the patient's colon was not suitably prepared for the examination. Desirable testing is not enough; it must also be done properly.

Case 106. When performing an abortion, the physician discovered minimal amounts of tissue remaining. He failed to repeat suction, and this led to complications, litigation, and an award of damages.

Case 107. Not being well informed is an obvious way that doctors and their personnel can get into trouble. A 36-year-old pregnant patient, concerned about possible genetic defects of her child, asked for amniocentesis. The nurse discouraged the woman by stressing the risks of the procedure, and the doctor insisted that amniocentesis was not needed until age 37. After the Down's syndrome baby was born, the parents sued the physician. He failed to know as much as his patient in this instance, something that is legally and professionally indefensible.

Case 108. Another pregnant woman did her part by reporting a lump in her breast. A surgeon diagnosed it as benign, but when the lump enlarged, a biopsy revealed a malignancy. The patient died when the baby was one year old. In approving a large award of damages, the court noted that the obstetricians involved had available to them mammography, thermography, sonography, and needle aspiration to assist their diagnosis, but availed themselves of none of them.

Case 109. Failure to do a Pap test led to a huge award of damages in this case. A 38-year-old woman complained of excessive menstrual bleeding. An obstetrics-gynecology specialist prescribed Provera, but did not do a Pap test. The treatment worked for a few years, but when excessive bleeding recurred, a more complete examination revealed metastasized cancer. In the patient's lawsuit, it was recognized that failure of the doctor to do a Pap test was below the applicable standard of care. The test could have detected the cancer at a preinvasive stage.

Case 110. When a patient reported breathlessness after climbing stairs, the cardiologist did a treadmill test, diagnosing the problem as silent angina. He prescribed a vasodilator, a beta blocker, and a calcium blocker. The patient subsequently took one vasodilator capsule, collapsed, and spent several days in an intensive care unit. He had arrived with symptoms resembling a heart attack. He recovered when all medications were stopped. Subsequent tests showed no angina and no heart damage, but just a strong reaction to the medication. The overdose could have been avoided by doing titration or otherwise easing the patient into the potent drug regimen.

Case 111. A patient asked her physician to do a pregnancy test and examine a rash. She was found to be pregnant and the rash was diagnosed as roseola. However, the physician failed to take blood samples or run rubella titer tests. By the time the physician referred the patient to an obstetrics-gynecology specialist, the period for proper testing for rubella had passed and the tests proved inconclusive. The rubella led to the birth of a child with severe congenital defects. The parents sued the original physician, stating that they would have opted for an abortion if they had known of the rubella. Damages were awarded.

Case 112. This is the simplest case of all. The patient complained of pain and a tiny lump in her breast. Her doctor told her to stop worrying about it. Seven months later, the size of the lump and intensity of the pain had increased. Another physician ordered a mammogram, and cancer was found. A mastectomy was performed, but terminal illness developed. Expectedly, the first physician was sued.

Reassuring patients has its merits, but only if the doctor

has good reason for optimism. He does no favors for his patients by relieving them of worries without being reasonably certain that their concerns are unfounded.

Case 113. Finally, on this issue, failure to order a pregnancy test before doing a hysterectomy meant that the patient lost a two-week-old fetus. She sued the doctor, whose defense counsel was in a most unenviable position.

Complete Medical History Information Not Obtained

Before going on to diagnose or treat a patient, the practitioner is expected to obtain all the pertinent information needed to proceed. Failure to do so may mean that erroneous decisions will follow, with potentially catastrophic consequences for the patient and malpractice liability for the doctor.

Case 114. Whether the patient had eaten shortly before anesthesia was given had not been determined. She died under anesthesia while giving birth. The physician and hospital shared responsibility and contributed to settlement of the malpractice claim.

Case 115. Similarly, a patient was given general anesthesia prior to surgery to repair a lacerated finger. He had eaten five hours before the anesthesia was administered, but no one had inquired about it. He vomited during surgery and was given more thiopental sodium. Afterward, there was cardiac arrest, and the patient died. The hospital and anesthesiologist in this case shared the malpractice claim settlement.

Case 116. After the patient suffered a reaction to a contrast dye used in a radiologic diagnostic test, there was a review by the parties involved. Should the consent process have included a warning about rare reactions of this kind? Should the patient have been carefully observed to determine whether there was a reaction? Pertinent to our interest was concern over whether the radiology department should have taken a medical history to try to ascertain the risk of allergic reaction by the patient. It might have helped in this instance.

Case 117. The patient had had a previous episode of gastrointestinal bleeding. An anti-inflammatory medication was prescribed for a knee problem. The medication can cause gastrointestinal bleeding in one who is susceptible. By failing to inquire about the patient's past history, the prescriber chose an inappropriate anti-inflammatory drug, which ultimately led to the loss of part of the patient's stomach. The malpractice suit was settled for a sizable sum.

Case 118. The patient had heart disease and was in need of a stress test in order to apply for Social Security disability benefits. His prior medical record was not obtained; therefore, those doing the stress test were unaware of the patient's history of two myocardial infarct episodes and severe angina. Two stress tests were given within four weeks. In neither case was the possibility of a stroke mentioned in the consent form or in an oral explanation. The patient did have a stroke and lost his eyesight as well.

Suit was filed and negligence was found in administering a stress test without consulting the medical record. The award of damages was very substantial.

Failure to Obtain Consultation

In a medical world of growing specialization, a general practitioner is at risk of malpractice liability if he does not call in a specialist to consult on problems with which the generalist may not be completely familiar or fully competent. One specialist may need to inquire of a specialist in another field, too, when the patient has a problem outside of the initial specialist's realm of technical knowledge.

Case 119. A general surgeon diagnosed a child as having an indirect hernia. Although the surgeon did little pediatric surgery, he proceeded to do so here and discovered a direct hernia. Also, he inadvertently cut the bladder. He then reoperated a number of times without seeking specialty consultation. The child suffered kidney failure and won a huge settlement in his malpractice claim.

Here we have a misdiagnosis due to lack of expertise in the area, compounded by a surgical error, and magnified by efforts to correct the problem without the aid of a more skilled specialist.

Case 120. A 10-year-old girl was brought to a pediatrician's office with a two-day-old bump on her head. No trauma was involved. A physician at an x-ray laboratory read the x-ray as normal. Three months later, the bump had doubled in size and x-rays were taken at a different laboratory. This time the reading was "old hematoma with calcification." In another three months, the patient was seen by the pediatrician for fever, but not examined for the growing lump. Finally, in another three months, she was examined at a medical school hospital, and the lump was diagnosed as cancerous. The original pediatrician offered to be of assistance to the child and her mother and to cancel all old bills. Nevertheless, suit was filed.

Medical experts reviewing the case felt that the child should have been referred to a specialist just as soon as the growing lump, without traumatic causation, was identified.

Case 121. An auto accident victim was x-rayed in the emergency room and found not to have any spinal fractures. He returned four hours after being released, when deficits in the lower extremities were noted. The hospital staff contacted the patient's family physician to arrange for further care. The bad result, it turned out, was due to two spinal fractures. It was alleged that had a neurologist been called instead of a family practitioner, the resulting quadriplegia might have been avoided. A very large settlement of the patient's suit against the hospital was arranged.

Case 122. A young man complained of gastrointestinal problems. An upper G.I. series and a sigmoidoscopy were done. Unfortunately, a correct diagnosis of Crohn's disease was much delayed. So the patient sued the slow-diagnosing physician, alleging that if a gastroenterologist had been called in a timely manner, the proper diagnosis would have been made more quickly. The settlement was for a modest amount plus the cost of subsequent treatment of Crohn's disease.

Case 123. The referring physician may have a responsibility of not only referring the patient to a specialist but also of referring him to a second such specialist if the first one is unsuccessful in caring for the patient. That is what happened when a diabetic patient was referred to an orthopedic surgeon for an injured foot. Soaking the foot in antiseptic solution was suggested. Gangrene developed and amputation followed. The orthopedist settled with the patient, but the referring family physician also was sued on the theory that upon learning of the orthopedist's treatment, or upon asking the patient about it, he should have referred the patient to another orthopedic specialist before it was too late to save the foot. The patient also obtained a settlement from the family doctor.

Case 124. A general practitoner was caring for a pregnant patient. Her twins were born prematurely and one suffered a hemorrhage, cerebral palsy, and mental retardation. The parents sued their doctor for allegedly negligent prenatal care. Although they did not win an award, the parents' suit demonstrated the wisdom of referring problem obstetrical cases to a specialist, thus avoiding the risk of being inadequate to the task.

Case 125. The physician had been disciplined at the hospital for performing craniotomies on patients whose brain tissue samples did not indicate need for such surgery.

It was agreed that he would consult with an outside pathologist and also have x-rays interpreted before doing any future craniotomies. The doctor did not abide by the agreement, which simply reflected basic good practice, and did surgery without the required specialty consultation. A jury verdict against the hospital and physician led to the doctor's being compelled to reimburse the hospital for a judgment brought against it, since the hospital's conduct was appropriate and not negligent.

Laxity in Follow-up Care

It is a truism that the physician's task, especially if the physician is a surgeon, continues during the full extent of the follow-up or posttreatment period. Failure to provide the necessary continuity of care is malpractice if it is inconsistent with the applicable professional standard of care.

Case 126. A 20-year-old unwed patient had an abortion at eight weeks of pregnancy, plus a D and C procedure. The pathologist reported that no products of conception had been removed. Therefore, if the patient really was pregnant, she continued to be. The patient had no postabortion follow-up visits and had an unwanted baby. She sued the abortion physician who, it turned out, never noticed what the pathologist had reported. Although the patient must have realized at some stage that the abortion had not been successful, she did not initiate follow-up medical care. However, she did file suit.

Inasmuch as the defendant physician had neither read the pathology report nor maintained any postabortion contact with the patient, he was vulnerable in court and arranged a pretrial settlement.

Case 127. A physician prescribed Prednisolone for arthritis. The patient took the drug for two years and allegedly became addicted to it because the prescription had been refilled some 42 times, 23 of them as approved by the physician or by his personnel when phoned by the pharmacist. The doctor's records showed that only one refill was permitted by the original prescription. However, he did recall authorizing refills via the telephone a few times. Both the prescribing physician and pharmacy were sued.

The physician evidently was aware that the patient was continuing to take the drug long after it was first prescribed. He should have contacted the patient to determine whether it was doing any good or harm. At least that would have been the malpractice theory if the suit had come to trial.

Case 128. For many years, a radiologist had been doing an annual chest x-ray of the patient, reporting the results to her and her physician. One year the radiologist failed to report on his reading of the x-ray. Neither the patient nor her physician inquired about the missing annual report but, as it happened, the x-ray revealed a tumor that proved to be malignant. A lawsuit followed. The radiologist could not escape his responsibility for failing to follow up the x-ray with a report even though the patient was somewhat lax in not making a timely inquiry.

Case 129. In the course of doing a flight physical examination, the physician used Hemoccult Developer in the patient's eyes instead of Ophthetic, either due to mislabeling or negligent storage procedures. This was unfortunate enough, but failure of follow-up meant that timely remedial measures were not taken.

A lawsuit was pursued by the patient, whose impaired eyesight meant he no longer could be a private pilot.

CHAPTER FIVE

Inattention to and Abandonment of Patients

ONCE THE PHYSICIAN or health care provider commences the doctor-patient relationship, there is an obligation to continue with necessary care until the patient has recovered, withdraws from the relationship, is transferred to another health care professional or facility that is both competent to care for him and accepts him for such care, or the patient dies. To accept a patient and then cease to provide needed care may constitute abandonment. This form of malpractice can carry with it a serious risk of liability.

Related to abandonment is inattention to the patient's perceived needs, premature cessation of physician contact and interest, turning the patient over to less qualified care givers, and failure to extend concern for the patient's fears or misunderstandings, whether they are justified or not.

Curtailing physician interest may not be stated as a cause of action in a lawsuit, but it may well be a major factor in turning the patient against the provider and removing inhibitions to litigation. Rarely given as a charge in a lawsuit is that the physician continued to bill although the patient did not have a good result and that the physician did not make follow-up inquiries to ascertain the patient's condition. To the patient, this may appear to be evidence of the doctor's greater interest in payment than in the patient's welfare. To the doctor, this is just an efficient business practice. Bills must be sent if they are to be paid; the doctor is busy enough without wasting time calling patients who, when last seen, seemed to be doing satisfactorily. After all, most patients who aren't well will contact the doctor. Unfortunately, that is not always true. Furthermore, when the patient has paid with his own money, and may be personally obligated to pay future medical bills, there may be a reluctance to recontact the physician. To protect himself from unnecessary exposure to litigation, the physician should have a follow-up procedure. This may prevent the charge of inattention or abandonment.

Legal Theory of Abandonment

The legal theory of abandonment is based primarily on the contractual relationship between doctor and patient. A breach of the obligation does not require expert medical witnesses for proof of the offense in court. Hence, it is easier to prove than conventional professional negligence (although it may also be considered to be such negligence). Especially to be avoided is the situation in which the physician refuses to continue to care for the patient because the latter could not give assurances of ability to pay for the care or to clear up prior indebtedness. Even if the reason for terminating care is lack of cooperation of the patient, an abrupt cessation of the doctor-patient relationship is fraught with risk. There are proper, protective ways of ending the relationship by arranging for competent care elsewhere or by giving the patient ample notice and suggesting sources of likely care givers.

In a genuine emergency, the physician may have to keep one patient waiting because another is in much greater need. The difference in urgency had best be obvious, though. Having more patients than can be treated may not be an effective defense. After all, the physician does not have to accept new elective patients who cause him to be overextended. However, his existing patients, especially those in the midst of a course of treatment, have a higher priority and may have a claim of abandonment if the busy doctor ignores them. A really overburdened doctor may even agree to accept a new patient only for the particular medical problem of the moment, with the understanding that there will not be a continuing relationship thereafter.

Among situations that have been categorized as abandonment have been these: inadequate postoperative follow-up; failure to make a home visit to an incapacitated patient; engaging a "ghost" surgeon without the patient's knowledge or consent; delegating treatment to an unqualified office assistant; and curtailing care for a suspected hypochondriac. Transferring a patient to a facility less capable of rendering care, primarily because of the patient's unpaid bills, is clearly risking an abandonment charge.

Physician-Patient Relationship

How does a physician terminate a patient relationship safely? The trick is to select a nonemergency situation and advise the patient that it would be best for both if the patient were treated by others. This conversation should be recorded in a letter to the patient. This letter should include an offer to continue care for a reasonable period (probably no less than a week), to direct the patient to sources of information about care givers (perhaps the county medical society), and to forward the patient's medical records to the new practitioner. If a reason is given in the letter for terminating the relationship, disregard of medical advice rather than nonpayment of bills should be relied upon. Where the physician is a specialist and the only one around, he may be unable to terminate the relationship.

Emergency rooms are presented with ample opportunity to reject patients who seem unable to pay for treatment.

This is a highly dangerous situation. To reject a patient who then dies or has a seriously negative outcome is to invite litigation. The hospital must at least stabilize the patient before arranging to send him to another provider or institution that has agreed to take him or is obligated by law to do so.

When the patient appears with no evidence of ability to pay, or with indications of membership in a health plan that inadequately compensates nonparticipating providers, there is risk in not offering all the care needed to stabilize the patient before referring him to another willing provider.

Abandonment or Delegation of Care

Following are some recent real cases that raise the issue of abandonment or delegating care to nonphysicians.

Case 130. Metal staples were used to suture a hysterectomy patient. During the postoperative period, the patient had some complaints. They were assumed to be normal for such a posthysterectomy case, but upon retrospective review the physician's behavior appeared to be inattentive or unresponsive. Failure to listen to the patient may have been the major reason for her malpractice suit, not any problem with the staples.

Case 131. The physician's concern for the patient's limited income, and possibile inability to pay for surgery, may have caused the physician to delay informing the patient about her cancerous eyelid. It was not until six weeks after receiving the pathologist's report that the physician advised the patient of the findings. If it were disclosed to a jury that his delay was because he might have to perform the procedure and not be paid for it, punitive damages might have been assessed in addition to compensatory damages.

Case 132. The patient had a vasectomy. He indicated to his doctor that his postoperative recovery was proceeding uneventfully. In fact, however, he had an infection that later led to the loss of a testicle. The patient had not wanted to come to the physician's office because it was somewhat inconvenient. Had the physician insisted upon such a visit because of a suspicion that all was not going well, he may have avoided the bad result and lawsuit. The charge of disinterest during the postsurgical period became credible in retrospect; consequently, the suit was settled rather than risk a jury's reaction.

Case 133. An obstetrician-gynecologist was willing to volunteer in the hospital emergency room, whose chief decided the man was competent to handle burn cases. He was not. A burn patient developed tetanus and died. The emergency department chief was unsuccessful in escaping potential liability because he had assigned a physician who was untrained in treating major burn injuries to serve the patient. Such an assignment is related to abandonment and risks an award of substantial damages.

Case 134. A dental patient was scheduled to have 11 teeth extracted. The dentist chose general anesthesia. The patient was attended by an untrained office assistant who was unable to cope when the patient stopped breathing. An ambulance crew revived the patient with cardiopulmonary respiration, but he died 10 days later. Liability exposure was clear because the practitioner used (abandoned his patients to) unqualified personnel in providing general anesthesia in his office practice.

Case 135. A somewhat similar case occurred when an aged patient was to have an eye examination because of glaucoma. She was given eyedrops, causing blurred vision. She then fell in the office, fractured her hip, and underwent hip replacement procedures.

In the lawsuit that followed, the court took cognizance of the fact that the opthalmologist's "nurses" were persons with no medical training whatsoever. Therefore, the patient who was left with them was essentially unattended. This delegation of responsibility by the doctor to untrained assistants—abandonment—led to a significant damage award.

Case 136. A casual approach to postoperative problems caused a malpractice claim against two physicians. The 26-year-old patient had an abortion, then a postoperative infection, followed eventually by a hysterectomy. The doctor did not answer the patient's phone calls or agree to an office visit the patient requested. The doctor's partner did respond to the patient's call, prescribing antibiotics—which proved to be ineffective—without seeing the patient. The patient eventually went elsewhere, but too late to avoid the hysterectomy and its sterilization effect.

Review of this case indicates abandonment. The nonresponsive physician was exposed to liability with little chance of a successful defense. One suspects that the young woman, who was unwed, was considered neither a good patient nor a reliable payer of medical bills. It was a mistake to treat her so cavalierly.

Case 137. As stated elsewhere, much medical care is accomplished by telephone; the risks inherent in this practice are recognized and are accepted as unavoidable. There are, however, some chances of error via a telephone response that are beyond the point of acceptable risk. Consider this incident: The physician had called in a prescription to the pharmacy for Elavil, 150 mg capsules. The pharmacy put the correct medication in the container but erroneously labeled it as containing 25 mg capsules. The patient noticed the discrepancy and phoned the prescribing physician. He advised his nurse to tell the patient to take six capsules instead of one each time. The resulting overdose led to hospitalization. The patient sued the pharmacy which, in turn, sued the doctor as the one whose action in advising the patient was the proximate cause of the overdose.

The doctor "shot from the hip" instead of displaying more cautious, professional behavior. He should have checked with the pharmacy and/or examined the medication before telling the patient how many capsules to ingest.

Case 138. Lack of candor and follow-up resulted in a lawsuit against radiation therapists. Their patient was to have received 30 treatments but, after 25, therapy was stopped abruptly. The patient was denied an explanation as to why therapy was terminated. His condition deteriorated. Just before he died, about a year after the radiation treatments ended, he learned that others had received excess radiation from the same source. The patient's cystitis and proctitis were linked to the radiation overdose when a consultant discovered that a gross miscalculation had caused excessive exposure, far greater than called for in the treatment plan. The patient's widow filed suit, and the radiologists, who refused to communicate and took no follow-up action, were at risk of punitive damages for their unprofessional conduct.

Case 139. How to escape a charge of abandonment is taught by this case. The patient had been admitted to a hospital after complaining of rectal bleeding. Although scheduled for surgery, she refused to sign a consent form. The physician, deciding to disassociate himself from the patient, gave her a list of other doctors whom she might contact to provide further care. She chose one who was unable to attend her for at least three days. Therefore, she left the hospital on her own volition and later sued the first physician and hospital for abandoning her. Two courts concurred that since the patient was not in urgent need of care, it was reasonable to present her with a list of prospective doctors. To do so was not abandonment. However, applying hindsight, it might be suggested that the first physician should have continued to provide care until his replacement took over so that there would be no gap in continuity of care.

CHAPTER SIX

Personal Problems of Practitioners and Their Employees

IN ANY GROUP of Americans, it can be assumed that a certain percentage are impaired because of emotional conditions or abuse of alcohol or drugs. It should not be expected that physicians, hospital personnel, and other health care workers are excluded from this reality. In fact, the problem may be worse among these groups because of stressful working conditions and ready access to mood-altering or pain-relieving substances. Estimates that 5 to 10 percent of the nation's physicians are incompetent or impaired have surfaced from time to time, but such estimates may simply be based upon normal distribution in the population.

Certainly, nowhere near that many physicians are subject to disciplinary action by state medical licensing agencies, medical societies, or hospitals. The profession in many locations has taken seriously its obligation to protect the public by limiting or terminating the right to practice by incompetent or impaired physicians. In some states, the disciplinary process is beginning to be effective. In addition to investigating reports of incompetent physicians and disturbed or addicted doctors, many state agencies and medical societies have programs for arranging treatment for impaired physicians so that they are enabled to return safely to practice.

Incidence of Impairment

At some time, it has been estimated, as many as one of eight American physicians will suffer from alcoholism, drug addiction, or psychiatric disorders during their professional lifetimes. Added to this risk is the potential for other impairments such as neurological disabilities, physical problems, and senility. Any physician so affected has a potential for committing medical malpractice far greater than does the unimpaired practitioner. Unfortunately, the affected individual is less likely to be aware of his diminished ability to practice safely if he is incompetent or impaired. Therefore, others must identify the problem practitioner and set in motion a procedure to protect the public from the enhanced risk of malpractice represented by the impaired person.

Avoiding Practice While Impaired

Doctors should be capable of adopting certain rules of personal conduct to assist in avoiding committing malpractice due to use of alcohol or drugs. To treat patients while under the detectable influence of these substances is a known risk. The doctor should do whatever is possible to avoid treating patients while "under the influence." Even if he does not commit malpractice in the legal sense, if the patient experiences a bad result and can show that the doctor was under the possible impairment of alcohol or drugs, a jury would likely find professional negligence (malpractice). The risk of malpractice liability is bad enough without enhancing it in this way.

To be sure, a doctor who takes drugs or relies upon alcohol may be doing it in order to be able to face his professional demands. He may feel that he cannot see all those patients without help from his crutch, the substance. Consequently, to tell such a person that when he is using drugs or alcohol he should refrain from seeing patients often is unrealistic. Such a practitioner must be prevented from seeing patients until achieving a substance-free condition.

A doctor who is having domestic problems may be so upset that his professional judgment is impaired. A disturbed, angry, despondent, or worried doctor is ripe for judgmental errors. Such a practitioner must somehow allow more time to make decisions concerning patients in order to be certain that his full intellectual capacity has been devoted to the professional decision-making.

A personality defect that reflects itself in the abuse of patients is the one that propels practitioners to have sexual affairs with patients, usually described as part of a "treatment." The problem is seen primarily among psychotherapists. One reported survey of psychiatrists revealed that 6 percent of those surveyed admitted having sexual relations with patients in spite of the Hippocratic oath and the ethical principles of the American Psychiatric Association. Not only male therapists are involved: Three percent of female psychiatrists surveyed have acknowledged having sexual contacts with their patients.

The ability to defend a malpractice suit in these situations is very limited. Although the patient may be labeled as disturbed—a psychiatrist's patient, no less—and therefore not fully credible, such patients have done quite well in court.

Practitioner's Undesirable Personal Behavior

In a random survey of malpractice situations involving undesirable personal behavior on the part of the practitioner, these appeared:

Case 140. A psychiatrist engaged in sexual relations with his patient, insisting that it was part of her therapy. The treatment apparently did not improve the patient's mental or physical health, and she sued the therapist. His behavior was malpractice according to the ethical principles of the American Medical Association and American Psychiatric Association. At issue, however, was whether the doctor's malpractice insurance carrier had to defend him. The policy did not cover intentional torts such as assault and battery. It was determined that the doctor's conduct could be considered just plain medical malpractice. Therefore, the carrier had the obligation to defend him. If punitive damages were awarded, however, the carrier would not be obligated to pay them. As is customary, that was excluded from the policy's protection and would be the personal responsibility of the insured doctor.

Case 141. The patient was experiencing dysmenorrhea. Having found no reason for it, the doctor conducted a gynecological examination consisting of stimulating the patient's genitalia, without explaining what he was doing, and why, and over her protests. The doctor told her to relax and think of her husband and then proceeded to do what he intended.

The subsequent lawsuit was based on alleged posttraumatic syndrome, as if the patient had been raped. Her psychic injuries were credible enough, in addition to the doctor's indefensible conduct, to compel a very substantial settlement. Clearly, a male doctor doing a gynecological examination should have a female nurse or attendant present for his protection and to reassure the patient.

Case 142. A psychiatrist was providing psychotherapy to a lesbian patient. Part of his therapy was fornication with her. She sued for assault as well as malpractice. His insurer refused to defend him because it felt that what he did was neither the practice of medicine nor substandard medical practice (malpractice), therefore it was not professional activity and was not insured. The court agreed, adding that public policy forbids the use of insurance to pay for the cost of illicit or immoral activities. So the doctor was on his own in defending against the patient's suit and in paying any resulting judgment award.

Inappropriate Behavior by Personnel

At a lesser level of personal offense is the engaging of personnel who, in their contact with patients and others, are rude, uninformed, indiscreet, or just plain unintelligent. Even well-paid employees can be guilty of these failings. Rarely do their indiscretions or failings appear in malpractice claims as an identified cause of the suit. Nevertheless, improper behavior by physician's personnel can start a chain of thought or circumstances that ends up in court.

Employees must be more than cautioned to maintain the patient's confidentiality; they should be trained specifically, with examples given of "do's and don'ts." They are not to personally diagnose or treat patients, over the phone or in person. They should not keep patients waiting for lengthy periods on the phone. Nor are they to assume the role of gatekeeper in order to protect the doctor from direct contact by the patients.

What the doctor fails to hear from the patient may lead to a malpractice situation. Here is a pertinent real case:

Case 143. The doctor entrusted his office employee to file pathologist's reports as to cancer. She failed to note that the pathologist had indicated the need for a six-month follow-up for the patient. Then, when the alert laboratory sent the doctor a reminder at the six-month point, the same employee pulled the file of another patient with a somewhat similar name who had had a hysterectomy and thus needed no further Pap tests. So the real patient was not contacted. She appeared in another six months, was tested, and was found to have cancer. It had spread, and she died seven months later at age 27.

A lawsuit was filed and tried. The doctor's defense was that entrusting office personnel in this manner was the standard in the medical community and, therefore, the unfortunate developments were not the result of any substandard practice. Had he engaged a more trustworthy employee, he would have escaped frightening litigation that went on for many years.

Communications may be even more important in the hospital setting, where there are so many employees who may have contact with patients and their families; furthermore, the more serious medical problems are handled in hospitals. It is well understood that certain matters require delicacy. Requesting authorization for an autopsy is one. Seeking organs for transplantation is another. Consider this example:

Case 144. Two babies were sent home from a hospital in the hands of the wrong parents. One set of parents announced, after the children were restored to their proper homes, that they intended to sue the hospital. They told the press that their anger was aroused by the hospital's administrator, who acted as if the babies were merely objects. "It was just like he was saying, 'I'm sorry we gave you the wrong toaster,' " one mother declared to the press. The other couple was miffed but had not yet indicated any intentions of filing suit for negligent infliction of emotional injury. Surely, in such a circumstance, the administrator could have developed a manner of communication that exhibited genuine concern for the anguish the parents had experienced because of the error of hospital personnel.

There are no statistics to show how many malpractice claims have been triggered by curt treatment of patients or their families, impersonal contacts, and overly businesslike communications. There are data about the incidence of suits against small-town family practitioners, however. Patients do not often consider suing a doctor who is a friend, who seems to care, and who is solicitous about the patient's welfare, even if there is a bad result (and there was malpractice). The impersonal relationship between doctor and patient, because of urban conditions or the rise of medical specialization, must have made a substantial contribution to the ease with which Americans file malpractice actions.

Collection Matters

Aggressive billing practices, when a patient turns out to have been dissatisfied with the medical services or the result, can set off a disaffection that ends in malpractice litigation. What may have been, at most, an uncollected patient's bill, may prove to be a big bill for the doctor in defending a lawsuit. Consequently, it should be determined before turning over a bill to a collection agency (or pursuing vigorous collection efforts by the provider's own office) that the services rendered were appropriate, properly done, and that the patient had a satisfactory outcome. If negative factors are found, direct contact between doctor and patient may be the better wisdom prior to going further with collection measures.

Choosing a collection agency can be a critical decision. Since the collector usually is compensated on a commission basis, its incentives are to pressure the debtor by whatever means (that are not criminal, prohibited by law, or likely to be discovered) will achieve payment. The collection agency is not much concerned with why the bill has not been paid, nor does it want the patient to pay the doctor directly at that stage. It wants to be responsible for accomplishing payment, and it could easily overstep the bounds of propriety in the process. The doctor may be judged by the antics of the collection agency he has chosen and will be the recipient of animosity aimed at the overaggressive collector.

The inevitable long wait in the outer office by patients with appointments can backfire, too. The patient who must wait most of the time may feel that his concerns are given a low priority by the doctor. The combination of having to wait routinely, receiving care that is not completely effective, being treated impersonally, and then facing persistent billing efforts contributes to a recipe for malpractice readiness. This is especially so when the patient has not been prepared for the size of the bill.

CHAPTER SEVEN

Inhospital Malpractice Prevention

THE BULK of malpractice suits concern incidents that have occurred at a hospital, although the primary defendant may well be a physician. Certainly, the major risks are cases involving inhospital events. Therefore, risk management at the hospital level may be the most potentially rewarding activity in the prevention of malpractice and suits alleging that malpractice has been committed.

Hospital Risk Management Programs

Risk management is a systematic approach—an early warning system—intended to identify situations that constitute malpractice or practices that could lead to compensable events within the hospital. Use of incident reports and other internal reporting methods is a way of identifying potential malpractice situations while the patient is in the hospital or after his discharge. Chart review is another mechanism for identifying occurrences that were substandard, irrespective of whether any patient harm resulted. Discovering bad practices and addressing them is a means for preventing malpractice, in contrast with reacting to it after a patient has been hurt.

Early discovery of a potential malpractice claim affords

the opportunity to decide whether to discuss the matter with the patient or his family. By initiating such conversations, medical and hospital representatives oftentimes may develop a rapport that discourages litigation even by those who have been victimized by substandard care. There is risk in telling the patient what he might never learn otherwise, possibly prompting a suit thereby, but it is a chance worth taking in many situations. Before going to the patient in such instances, the hospital will have collected useful information in a timely manner; for this reason, it will be in a better position to defend a malpractice suit if the patient does sue.

FLORIDA STATUTORY REQUIREMENTS

In Florida, state law already requires hospitals to implement internal risk management programs and specifies the tasks they are to carry out. In other states, hospitals would do well to consider voluntarily adopting programs that also feature collecting data on inhospital adverse incidents and analyzing the frequency and causes of these injurious incidents. Then the hospital must develop measures to minimize the chances of recurrence of these adverse incidents to patients, including "risk prevention" education and training programs for hospital staff. Expressed grievances by patients about their care should be analyzed. Furthermore, the incident reporting function should be made an affirmative duty of all hospital personnel and all providers of care in the facility. Submission of reports on cases of suspected injuries and adverse incidents to the hospital's risk manager should be mandatory.

The Florida law goes further in requiring the hospital to file a report with a state agency each year, telling of the number of incidents, listing the kinds of treatments causing injuries, naming the individuals responsible for the injuries, and describing malpractice suits filed and disciplinary actions taken against medical personnel as a result of injuries to patients. The sponsors of the legislation must have assumed that compulsory risk management programs would reduce the incidence of malpractice occurring within hospitals. Aside from the compulsory reporting to the state, which raises questions about breach of confidentiality and undue risk of liability for the named individuals and hospitals, the law may be of some benefit to the health field. Out of self-interest, of course, hospital management should need no statutory impetus to establish a program whereby adverse incidents are quickly identified and potentially risky practices are revealed and remedied.

FEDERAL REPORTING PROVISIONS

Enacted in late 1986, *The Health Care Quality Improvement Act of 1986* is aimed at improving the quality of medical care and reducing the incidence of malpractice. It applies throughout the country, but the extent of its benefits depend upon the individual hospital and its medical staff in meeting certain standards of peer review and whether the particular state chooses to add protections from state law actions to those already offered under federal law.

The statute is intended to restrict the ability of "incompetent physicians" to escape to another state without discovery of previous unacceptable performance. Additionally, it presumes that proper peer review can remedy some of the malpractice problem. To induce cooperation with the federal scheme, the act offers protection against federal antitrust suits brought by disgruntled physicians against hospitals and members of medical staff committees involved in peer review and physician discipline. The threat of such suits has deterred participation of some staff members in the peer review process and may discourage imposition of proper discipline in many cases.

Protection against federal antitrust lawsuits is already effective if the hospital peer review procedure meets federal statutory standards of due process or fair hearings. When disciplinary action is taken, beginning toward the end of 1987 the hospital must report it to the state board of medical examiners which, in turn, must report to a designated federal agency. Also, when a hospital or insurance carrier settles a malpractice claim or pays a judgment, it must report the details to the designated state and federal agencies or be subject to a fine. A hospital considering an application for staff privileges or renewal of privileges will have to ask the federal agency if there are any adverse reports about the physician, osteopath, or dentist.

The state medical licensing agencies also are required to report to the federal agency whenever they take punitive action against a physician.

In October of 1989, legal action for antitrust or other reasons, based on state law, will be barred against physicians conducting peer review as specified in the act. A state may accelerate the effective date or opt out of the statutory protection if its legislature so chooses.

The attractiveness of the federal bait should stimulate most hospitals in the country to adopt more effective peer review programs and make it difficult for physicians with bad malpractice experience or licensing problems to move readily to other hospitals or states.

Credentialing and Peer Review

A hospital has an opportunity at two different stages to protect itself against physician incompetence, lack of qualification, or personality problems. The first opportunity is when an application for staff privileges is reviewed, and subsequently, when the staff member is given an annual or biennial review. The second opportunity is when adverse incidents are reported. The easier solution to potential inhospital malpractice risks is the first—to exclude the malpractice-prone physician. Unfortunately, most malpractice is committed by apparently qualified practitioners whose record and behavior does not merit exclusion or disciplinary action. Nonetheless, careful scrutiny of all applicants for medical staff appointment can bar the more obvious malpractice risks, along with some others as well.

When reviewing applications for hospital staff membership, it is imperative to actually verify the applicant's medical school graduation, residencies, and licensure at the source. Accepting the applicant's word is simply not safe practice. Even more unreliable is a self-statement about prior staff privileges and whether such privileges or licensure have ever been suspended, reduced, or terminated. The hospitals and licensing agencies, especially those in other states, should be contacted directly to verify the applicant's statements. References should be contacted by telephone if a written letter from a reference is especially brief, unresponsive, or evasive.

Once appointed, a medical staff member should be subject to proctoring by qualified observers. The appointment should be provisional until satisfactory proctorship reports of a sufficient number of procedures have been prepared. All practitioners at the hospital should be required to show proof of current malpractice insurance coverage in amounts considered minimally adequate by the hospital. It is unfair to the institution and all of its practitioners to allow uninsured or underinsured staff members to practice in the facility and thus risk shifting the burden of liability to those who are properly insured. This is especially true when more than one defendant is named in a malpractice suit, which more often than not is the case.

Consider a recent revelation by the Veterans Administration, which operates the largest hospital system in the country. When the VA reviewed its medical staffs, it identified 93 doctors who had been previously disciplined by state medical regulatory agencies, including 24 whose licenses were at the time of the review suspended or revoked. The VA professed to be inadequately staffed and organized to be able to identify these physicians routinely. There had been no independent verification of the physicians' license status. After the VA inspector general audited the physicians' licenses due to concerns about the quality of care, the VA adopted a verification policy.

A study published in a prestigious medical journal reported that about one-fourth of doctors of all ages admitted to having recently treated themselves with mind-affecting drugs. This does not include self-treatment in order to stay awake. However, of the surveyed physicians, only one percent thought their use of drugs had caused them to give poor care to patients. Medical students and physicians under age 40 most frequently reported using these drugs. In addition to developing potentially dangerous personal habits, doctors who self-prescribe mood-altering drugs increase their chances of committing malpractice and make it difficult to defend against alleged malpractice if there is a bad result but no convincing proof of substandard care. Inhospital education programs are one way of delivering the message to practitioners that use of drugs, whether for recreational purposes or as a means of enabling them to carry on when they are too tired to remain alert, is an invitation to malpractice, inhospital discipline, and possibly the loss of medical licensure.

Case 145. The patient underwent three surgical procedures for subcutaneous mastectomy. They were poorly done by a surgeon who did not have proven qualifications to do them. The patient sued the hospital for allowing the doctor to perform procedures for which he was not qualified and because its nurses did not refuse to participate in surgery that was not medically indicated. The court recognized the patient's claim as stating a cause of action and permitted it to go to trial.

Hospital liability for not performing adequate inhouse peer review is a recognized legal risk. Therefore, physicians should be required to demonstrate their qualifications to perform particular procedures rather than being given blanket authorization in a particular specialty or subspecialty within the hospital.

There are many potential compensatory events that can be avoided by following sensible practices. A random selection of real malpractice cases produced numerous illustrations.

Poorly Transmitted Instructions to Personnel

Physicians give orders and hospital employees carry them out. These orders, except in urgent circumstances, should be in writing. But that is not enough if they are illegible, otherwise unclear, not timely, not self-limiting, or not understood.

Case 146. The patient's eye was injured when a tiny spring entered it. In the operating room, three medications were to be used. The physician, speaking through his mask, asked for Gentamicin and Solu-Medrol. Unfortunately, the technician, who had not prepared the medications, handed the doctor a syringe in which a form of cortisone not intended for internal use had been placed. The patient lost his chance to recover sight in the eye. Compounding the problem was the doctor's communicating through a mask to a foreign-born technician whose ability to clearly understand names of medications under the circumstances was subject to doubt.

The operating room technicians also should have followed a protocol to assure, in advance of need, that all medications to be used in the operating room were the ones indicated, rather than placing blind faith in the appearance of liquids.

Case 147. The patient entered the hospital for a left inguinal hernia procedure. However, hospital personnel had him sign a consent form for a right-side operation. The physician glanced at the consent form and operated on the right side, where he actually found a small hernia in the 77-year-old patient. Later, another surgeon repaired the left side hernia, and suit was filed against those involved in doing the original incorrect procedure.

The surgeon should have obtained a signed consent form himself and should not have relied upon hospital employees to do it for him. The hospital staff error could not have been corrected by the physician, since he was not fully familiar with what was required. Such impersonal relations with the patient made it impossible for the doctor to realize that an error had been made.

Case 148. The delivering obstetrician proceeded to do a circumcision only 24 hours after delivery even though the standard procedure was to wait a minimum of three days. The baby developed overwhelming sepsis and possibly residual urological problems. Had the standard procedure been made known to the doctor, or had he notified hospital personnel of his intention, they may have been able to stop the premature procedure. Certainly, review of any separate consent to circumcise might have triggered such intervention.

Case 149. Communications between physicians also must be clear and complete or serious harm can follow. For example, certain diabetic patients may react to the contrast medium used in radiologic procedures. The radiologist was unaware of the patient's diabetic state and medical history prior to using the I.V. contrast material.

The patient sued the hospital and the hospital-based radiologist after suffering renal failure. Investigation revealed that the referring physician had indeed advised the radiology technician that the patient was a diabetic and that the contrast material should not be used. However, when the patient's appointment date was rescheduled, this information was not re-recorded. The patient was not aware that he should not have been given the contrast medium. The hospital settled the claim, since its employee, the technician, had erred in losing the vital information and instruction.

Case 150. At issue was the policy on fetal monitoring. The doctor had ordered removal of the monitoring device during labor, but did not order its reinstatement. Nursing personnel could have reinstituted the fetal monitoring if that was established hospital policy, or they might have brought the matter to the chief of the hospital department, if that was the policy. Where a policy is established, failure to carry it out, at the expense of the patient, means potential liability. Here, failure to do a cesarean section, perhaps because monitoring was absent, was blamed for the death of the infant at age two and led to settlement of the lawsuit.

Case 151. Hospital personnel incinerated a dead newborn, unaware that the parents had authorized an autopsy. They were concerned with whether the child had a chromosomal disorder or other hereditary defects. They expressed anticipational anxiety during the next pregnancy and made demand for compensation. Their claim was settled. If the parents' desire for an autopsy had been communicated to hospital personnel on time, this embarrassing incident would not have occurred.

Failure of Physician to Come to the Hospital

Absentee diagnosing and prescribing is known to have its risks, yet it must be resorted to because the doctor cannot dash over to the hospital every time he is called, especially when he is busy with other patients or is far away. Nevertheless, he must realize the exposure to risk whenever he opts to not come to the hospital to see his patient.

Case 152. A compliant physician who allowed his name to be used as admitting physician for a drug addict at the request of a drug rehabilitation center later suffered the agony of a lawsuit. It seemed that the doctor was ill and agreed to admit the patient only if he did not have to attend him. The patient died within four days from meningitis, which was not diagnosed until a day before his death. The court refused to dismiss the suit against the doctor because he appeared to have been negligent in accepting a patient unseen, then not diagnosing him and thus possibly contributing to the death. Had the doctor come to the hospital, his liability exposure would have been much reduced, and had he not accepted the case in absentia, there would have been no real risk of liability.

Case 153. A Jehovah's Witness had made it known that she would refuse blood transfusions under any circumstances. At the hospital, she was diagnosed as having a ruptured ectopic pregnancy requiring immediate surgery. The attending physician chose to wait 45 minutes for his partner to arrive and assist. The patient died of blood loss an hour or so thereafter. While her widower's suit failed on the issue of the failure to administer blood on his later authorization, a jury award was allowed by the court for the harm caused by waiting for the assistant physician to come to the hospital. The jury applied its powers of hindsight and decided that this delay was a major contributor to the patient's death.

It may be assumed that a physician who is too far from the hospital to come quickly enough to serve his patient when called, but has no arrangement for a closer substitute, is at legal risk. And the doctor who cannot be reached and has not arranged for a relief physician is equally vulnerable.

Failure to Promptly Record Necessary Information in the Medical Record

The medical record serves to provide all persons treating the patient with information they may need to know in order to make appropriate diagnostic and treatment decisions. The absence of pertinent information, either because it was never entered or because it was recorded too late to be useful, can lead to patient injury and malpractice litigation.

Case 154. There were two omissions of important information in the medical record of this case. The patient received no anesthesia in the operating room, but the physician assumed that he had. When the doctor learned of the omission, he made no entry to that effect. Then, 2.5 cm of a needle broke off and was left in the patient. The record contained no notations as to how long the search for the needle fragment went on or when an x-ray was taken in the course of the search. The operating physician was sued and held liable. The medical record was considered very suspicious because of absence of entries about the missing anesthesia and the attempt to retrieve the needle fragment.

Case 155. When there is no entry about a particular activity, a jury may assume that it did not take place. No fetal heart monitoring information appeared in the medical record in this case. The defective newborn's parents claimed that in absence of a tracing or any mention in the medical record of fetal heart monitoring, it may be assumed that there was none. The hospital representatives preferred to assume that there was only carelessness in recording what was done, but that is not very persuasive, especially when the injured party is an infant.

Case 156. The EKG results were not placed in the medical record before surgery commenced. Consequently, neither surgeon saw them and neither was aware of an abnormality prior to removing the gallbladder. During the operation, the patient suffered a massive heart attack and died. The hospital was held liable because the failure to post the EKG results was a breach of the accepted standard of care and contributed to the adverse result.

Case 157. If the medical record contains warning information, it must be heeded or those who do not must face the consequences. Here, the patient had surgery to remove a pituitary tumor. She was given intravenous ampicillin despite a chart entry indicating her allergy to penicillin. A cardiovascular collapse resulted, then a coma. Defense would have been difficult indeed in the ensuing lawsuit.

Altering Medical Records

One sure way to lose a malpractice suit is to go over the record and insert desirable information as if it were there all along. Worse yet is to obliterate, erase, or otherwise attempt to negate what was originally entered. Even though the motives are understandable—to add truthful information that should have been there, or to correct factual errors—the fact of the late entry or apparent attempt to change what was there may be assumed by the jury to indicate malevolence, guilt, or an attempt to make self-serving changes in vital documents.

The proper way to add information is to note that it is an addition. The date of entry should be honest. If it is a late entry, the reason for the delay should be stated and the entering practitioner's signature should follow. If an incorrect item has been entered, it should not be removed, crossed out, or otherwise altered. Rather, an additional entry should be made, including an explanation as to why different information is being recorded.

Case 158. A self-serving summary of the medical records of a newborn came to haunt the hospital two decades later. A two-page summary, released over the years in response to requests for medical record information, reported normal delivery and neonatal conditions. In fact, the delivery was by cesarean section, the baby was apneic at birth, and it developed to have an IQ of 25. More than 20 years later, a lawsuit was filed claiming prenatal brain damage. The suit was not barred by the statute of limitations because a newborn was involved, and there was apparent withholding of medical record information. A significant award was given to the now mature defective patient.

Failure to Obtain Peer Confirmation or Consultation

Hospitals should have rules and regulations for when consultations are required. Irrespective of those obligations, a physician should ask for confirmation of the diagnosis or plan of treatment when he is uncertain of his conclusions or when a specialist might have better insight. Not doing so is to risk liability when, in retrospect, it appears to laymen (such as jurors) that consultation likely would have prevented the misdiagnosis or ineffective or harmful treatment.

Case 159. A general surgeon experienced problems, and the operating room supervisor advised him to call in a vascular surgeon, since the general surgeon had no vascular surgery privileges at the hospital. The general surgeon persisted with the case, a bad result followed, and a malpractice suit was filed. Here, the surgeon went beyond his hospital privileges, which led to termination of his hospital appointment as well as the commencement of a malpractice suit.

Case 160. A podiatrist admitted a patient for heel surgery even though the hospital's bylaws required a joint admission with a physician. Prior to surgery, the patient was examined by a physician, but no medical doctor was involved in the patient's admission and care. A late-developing adverse result brought a suit against the hospital for allegedly failing to supervise the podiatrist or to enforce its own rules for admissions. Had the errant podiatrist sought professional assistance, there may not have been a bad result and the subsequent lawsuit.

Not Ordering Patient Restraints

Hospital rules may require certain restraints for patients whether or not they are specifically ordered by the attending physician. If there are such rules, they should be followed. If they are not, the patient who falls or crawls out of bed and is hurt will have an easily proven claim because hospital personnel failed to follow the institution's own rules. If there are no hospital rules, sometimes, when a doctor does not order restraints when indicated, the hospital may escape liability for the consequences but the doctor may not. It can be a mistake just to avoid annoying or insulting the patient, not to order restraints and permit the patient to harm himself. The hospital may be caught in a no-win situation if it receives no orders as to restraints, then assumes the doctor so intended, and the patient subsequently comes to grief. The hospital risks being held liable for not instituting restraints on its own as a safety measure, an action that is not dependent upon medical orders.

Case 161. The patient had vertigo, but his physician left no orders requiring restraints. The man fell while going to the bathroom without assistance. Although the patient could not induce any expert medical witnesses to testify on his behalf, the court decided that no expert witnesses were needed. Laymen can exercise their common knowledge in these simple situations without need of experts' assistance, the court said. Hospital and physician faced potential liability.

Case 162. A hospital was exposed to liability when a two-year-old patient fell out of a crib and broke an arm. Apparently, the crib side either did not catch when placed in an upright position or it was possible for a child to unlatch it. Either way, liability was inescapable. Better maintenance and nurse training were indicated.

Case 163. A stroke patient on many medications fell

out of bed twice. Neither time were bed rails raised. He suffered a broken leg, then amputation. The malpractice claim was settled, of course. In this case, properly adopted and enforced hospital rules might have precluded the indefensible inaction of hospital personnel.

Case 164. A spry 83-year-old patient left the bed more than once by going over the foot, despite warnings to first use the call button to summon assistance. The bed rails were up when she slipped on her own slipper and fractured a wrist. At issue was whether restraints should have been applied once the patient established that raised rails were ineffective to contain her. A conference with her doctor might have reduced the hospital's risk of liability if he insisted on no restraints despite the patient's penchant for mobility.

Case 165. A 77-year-old cataract patient wanted bathroom privileges, and her doctor approved. She fell in the bathroom, where no restraining belt was used. Despite the doctor's refusal to order restraints or assistance, hospital liability was likely when an elderly patient with vision in only one eye was allowed too much liberty. Therefore, the hospital settled the claim.

Case 166. An elderly, sedated patient fell out of bed when rails were not raised. The subsequent claim raised questions about whether the patient should have been given an orientation to the surroundings as a matter of routine practice, and whether bed rails should always be raised at night and also by day for heavily sedated patients. If imposed, these rules would be followed even in absence of doctor's orders regarding rails or restraints.

Improper Use of Medical Devices or Equipment

Inside a hospital are many devices and machines operated by hospital employees and by independent practitioners who enjoy staff privileges. The hospital has the obligation to maintain all such equipment in proper working order and is at risk if its personnel fail to use the devices at an acceptable level of competence. To the nonemployee practitioner there remains the risk of negligently operating the equipment in a way that causes harm to the patient. It is incumbent upon the physician to learn to use the machines competently even if it is not his obligation to vouch for their proper maintenance. Inspection and trial of the machinery before its use in a specific case may be required of the physician, if feasible, in order to satisfy the applicable standard of care.

Case 167. The patient might not have lived, or for very long, anyway, but he died on the operating table. The anesthesiologist, through "sheer habit," opened a valve she thought was oxygen but proved to be nitrous oxide. These valves were brightly color-coded. The reduced oxygen level proved fatal to the patient. Suit was filed against the anesthesiologist. The judge, in the belief that if there had been no negligence the patient might have survived a few years, suggested a settlement figure.

The machine here had no warning alarm when oxygen was limited but did signal if pressure dropped. An accessory device to provide such an alarm was available, but had not been acquired by the hospital. This could have constituted negligence on the part of the hospital if the accepted standard of care in the hospital community was to have anesthetic machines with these alarms. A hospital need not have the very latest equipment, but old, unsafe designs can be classified as substandard and may lead to liability.

Case 168. A surgeon, serving as first assistant in a coronary bypass operation, connected the heart-lung machine in such a way as to reverse the lines. Oxygen-depleted blood went to the brain, and irreversible brain damage resulted. He had failed to follow the medical group's practice of testing the equipment beforehand to verify that the lines are properly connected. If the lines are improperly connected and not tested, the damage is indicated on the monitors, but too late to reverse it. Failure to do the presurgical testing of the equipment led to a tragic result and a multimillion-dollar judgment award.

Case 169. Sometimes the improperly functioning machine gives warnings, but unless the warnings are correctly interpreted, it may be too late to avoid permanent injury to the patient. When a ventilator malfunctioned, it continued to cycle and increase its volume. This increase in volume was noticed but not properly interpreted as indicating that the ventilator was not connected to the endotracheal tube. The hysterectomy patient suffered brain damage and a seven-figure settlement was arranged.

Failure to Account for All Sponges and Instruments

One of the least defensible outcomes is when the patient emerges from surgery with a surgical sponge or instrument left in his body. In such a situation, the only justifiable reaction is to admit the error and make every effort to remove the foreign object from the patient's body as soon as is feasible. If the patient is not told of the problem, the statute of limitations will not run out, thus permitting the patient to bring suit when he does discover the negligence despite the passage of many more years than intended by the statute of limitations. A long delay in revealing to the patient that an item was lost also is likely to increase the amount of damages awarded.

Case 170. The patient's gallbladder was removed in 1968. Difficulties commenced in 1981 due to a sponge left within him at the time of the surgery. Eventually, extensive surgical repair was required. The lawsuit was filed more than 13 years after the initial operation, but the statute of limitations was tolled (suspended) for that time because the patient did not discover that he had been injured through the negligence of a lost sponge until 13 years later.

Case 171. The instrument count did not indicate that anything was missing, but the patient ended up with a "fish" (a metal ring with a tail string as a signal of its presence) inside him. In this instance, the tail somehow went into the abdominal area and ceased to be a reminder. Of course, the ring would have appeared in an x-ray had one been taken. The patient had to undergo additional surgery for removal of the lost "fish" and experienced a slow but successful recovery.

In some hospitals, although there is a sponge count, no instrument count is taken. This may be a calculated risk in order to avoid potentially harmful delay. Nevertheless, it is virtually indefensible, as the physician and his insurer in this case learned, when an instrument is left in the patient. Instrument counts are well worth adopting for the purpose of preventing malpractice claims.

Case 172. Sometimes even the best safety measures fail because of human inattention. Consider this situation: A laparotomy pad was left in the patient after emergency gallbladder surgery. The nurse's count was incorrect; however, an x-ray taken after surgery clearly showed the radiopaque strip in the pad. Whoever read the x-ray missed it. When complications developed, the patient sued and recovered a large judgment. Upon inquiry, it developed that the surgeon had seen the x-ray and misinterpreted the radiopaque strip as part of a Penrose drain that he assumed had been inadvertently left in the patient, yet he did not tell the patient about this, either. The amount of the award probably would have been much lower if the patient had been given prompt notice of the suspected foreign object left within him, even if it was misidentified.

Case 173. During insertion of a pacemaker, a scalpel handle was left inside the patient, necessitating another procedure to remove it. However, the second procedure had to be delayed because a postoperative infection developed from the foreign object. The attending physician or his assistants should have been aware of the missing scalpel handle.

This was one case where not informing the patient did not lead to even greater risk of liability. The patient, an elderly man, may never have learned of the real reason for the second procedure and therefore never sued. It represents one of the majority of cases of malpractice that do not result in claims. The option of not truthfully informing the patient should not be chosen, since it is unethical as well as likely to enhance the patient's injury and monetary damages if he does sue.

Premature Discharge, Especially for Financial Reasons

Providers of health care are pressured to avoid unnecessary diagnostic and treatment procedures for insured patients. They need no prodding about this when treating patients who appear to be unable to pay for their care, since the caregiver's incentives are weakened by the prospect of not being compensated.

In the hospital emergency room, there are decisions to be made when an uninsured patient appears and obviously will run up a huge bill if admitted. If he can be patched up and released, directed to another facility, or stabilized and transferred elsewhere, there may be avoidance of the economic problem. Such a practice may risk malpractice liability if the delay in treatment or failure to treat contributes to the patient's injury or condition. Recent instances in which hospitals, having failed to convince neurosurgeons and other specialists to come and treat apparently uninsured patients, sent the patients to distant public hospitals, where they died, have prompted remedial state and federal legislation.

A patient should not be discharged before he is ready, in the professional judgment of the attending physician, with consideration being given to the quality of care available at home or wherever the patient is going. Nor should emergency room cases be discharged until the medical risks are assessed. In transferring a patient to another hospital or referring him there, the other facility should be contacted to verify that it will accept the patient. The risk of deterioration of the patient's condition in the course of the transfer must be evaluated because it represents potential legal liability.

Case 174. A 13-year-old victim of an auto accident was stabilized in the emergency room and, because he seemed to be economically disadvantaged, was transferred to a county hospital. He had been seen in the emergency room by an orthopedic surgeon who recommended vascular surgery. Such a specialist was contacted by phone but not called in. The patient was presumed to have suffered aggravation of his injuries due to the time lost in making the transfer, thus delaying care by a qualified vascular surgeon.

Case 175. A slum dweller, shot during a dispute, remained in the local hospital emergency room for many hours. Efforts to induce the neurologists and related specialists on the hospital's list to come to the facility failed, probably because there was little prospect of payment the press reports later indicated. After hours of inquiry, the hospital was able to find a county institution willing to accept the patient, although it was a one-hour ambulance trip away. By the time the patient got there, he was virtually brain dead and died soon thereafter. His family engaged a prominent plaintiff's medical malpractice attorney to file suit and to publicize the case.

Case 176. The patient was on Medicare. The Medicare utilization review officer, not a physician, advised the patient's doctor that no extension of authorized stay in the hospital would be granted. With the patient's coverage of inhospital care about to expire, the doctor ordered her discharge. It proved to be premature, and the resulting consequences included rehospitalization and loss of a leg. The patient sued the state, whose Medicare agent, a nurse, following set guidelines and without seeing the patient, had refused to extend the Medicare coverage.

In the litigation that followed, the court explained that it is the attending physician's responsibility to assess the patient's need for hospitalization, irrespective of the insurance coverage. Premature discharge can be malpractice and is not excused by a decision, erroneous or not, by a third party as to payment for the health care services. It was the doctor's responsibility to appeal the Medicare decision and seek approval for payment of bills for additional hospital days, but either way, it was his professional obligation to order the necessary treatment.

Unfamiliarity with Drug Side Effects and Potentiation

It is perhaps unfair to expect the physician to be aware of all the significant potential side effects of prescription drugs or to know which combinations of individual drugs produce harmful effects not associated with one drug alone. Yet, the consequences of failing to be aware of these possibilities can be malpractice claims. The problem is aggravated when the patient receives many prescriptions, uses old drugs that the doctor doesn't know about, or indulges in doctor-shopping and obtains prescriptions from a number of physicians without their being aware of the prescribing by others. There are, of course, drug abusers who do this to support their habit, but they should be more readily identifiable by the kind of prescriptions they seek. The hypochondriac or worried unwell patient who is not drug dependent is the dangerous one because his antics may not be obvious. Sharp questioning may be the only way to detect the drug overutilizer. Full explanation of the potential side effects of the drug and dangers of combining drugs should be made. Warning labels should be ordered for the prescription container, and a note should be made in the medical record that the explanation was given. A typed warning, with a copy of it in the record, would be most helpful for future defense of the physician.

Case 177. A patient who had suffered a foot injury told the physician of his allergy to codeine. The pain-relieving medication given turned out to be a derivative of codeine. The patient suffered a reaction, including labored breathing and anxiety. The prescribing physician was sued. Since the patient did her part in announcing her allergy, she could be expected to prevail in her suit as against a prescriber who was unaware of the true content of the medication he prescribed and did not inform himself about it.

Gratuitous Criticism of Other Practitioners

Before the era of malpractice risk, it was not unusual to have a dentist look into the mouth of a new patient and exclaim, "Who did that to you?" There would follow an expensive correction of prior dental work. Among physicians, comments of this kind can drive the patient to sue the one who previously treated him. Not many of these incidents are revealed in the malpractice claims and suits, since the cause of action stated usually is the allegedly improper previous care, not the condemnatory remarks of the subsequent physician. Nevertheless, the manner of describing the prior medical judgment or service can incite a patient not only to blame a doctor but to sue him as the aftermath of a new physician's volunteered estimation of the quality of previous professional care. It is possible to word one's comments about previous professional work in a way that does not label it as malpractice.

Case 178. A physician removed a fibroadenoma from the patient's breast. Unfortunately, he failed to remove another lump at the same time. A month later, another physician removed the second lump. He noted in the medical record that the first "doctor forgot or neglected to remove the other fibroadenoma." The patient sued the forgetful doctor, armed with the second doctor's written accusation of professional negligence (malpractice). A settlement was reached. The medical record entry could have been worded in a way that would convey reality without also accusing the errant prior physician of malpractice.

Failure of Hospital to Record Maintenance Activities

We live in a paper world, but also an increasingly computerized world. If there is no record of an event, some people think it never happened, whatever it was. This concept haunts institutions as well as individual practitioners. If records do not show that equipment or facilities were inspected, adjusted, or routinely maintained, a jury may refuse to believe that the event occurred. This means that routine records are required of routine maintenance. Where calibration of equipment is at issue, the record of periodic inspection, adjustment, and repair is essential to demonstrate that these things were done. Consider the following simplistic example:

Case 179. A hospitalized patient fell while running. Why he was running is unclear. However, his claim alleged that the hospital floor was wet, slippery, or otherwise unsafe. The hospital had no records covering routine maintenance of floors and hallways, and consequently its ability to defend against the claim was hampered.

Utilization of Unlicensed or Unqualified Personnel

When hindsight is employed, what should have been done differently to prevent the untoward result to the patient is always perfectly clear. If the patient was cared for by someone who lacked a state license or was untrained in the particular activity, attention will focus on that individual. A hospital or doctor is at a distinct disadvantage in defending against a bad medical result if one of the major participants was not properly licensed or trained. To be sure, malpractice or negligence, even by a well-qualified and fully trained professional, is actionable. The problem is that if the substandard performance is by someone without these credentials, it is unlikely that a jury will even consider whether the performance may not have been below the applicable professional standard. A bad result of care by an unqualified person almost automatically calls for an award of some damages. Therefore, limiting the breadth of activity of unlicensed or inadequately trained personnel so as not to encroach upon the proper scope of practice of licensed personnel is imperative (except in genuine emergencies).

Case 180. Some 11 hours after labor commenced, a hospital nurse brought to the physician's attention the appearance of meconium-stained amniotic fluid. The doctor delayed surgical delivery until after 43 hours of unproductive labor. In the malpractice claim following the death of the baby, the doctor was at risk because of the decision to wait so long to do a cesarean section. The hospital could not escape potential liability, either, because the nurse was not licensed in the state. Her competence would be suspect, and the accuracy and timeliness of her reporting to the physician would be questioned.

Case 181. An intern was allowed to deliver a baby that was in a transverse lie and to use forceps to do so. This occurred in a county hospital. The mother was an unwed Mexican undocumented alien who subsequently never prosecuted a malpractice claim despite birth of a child with parietal fracture, facial palsy, basal skull fracture, and other defects. The intern sought no consultation until after the delivery. It appears that he was not qualified to handle a case of this difficulty without more experienced assistants.

Case 182. In most states, a nurse anesthetist must work under the authority and direction of a physician and administer anesthetics as ordered by him. In this case, there was no written order, and no physician was present as the nurse anesthetist administered a spinal anesthetic for a cesarean section. The patient had seizures and died, but the baby was rescued via emergency cesarean section. The widower and surviving children obtained an immense jury award from the anesthesia service that employed the anesthetist.

Case 183. In another nurse anesthetist case, the patient had been given five different drugs during a knee operation. After a spinal anesthetic, the patient, a 34-year-old woman, suffered slurred speech, incontinence, and blindness. It appeared that the spinal anesthetic administered by the nurse inadvertently caused a medical sympathectomy. The preoperative sedation also was excessive and the Pontocaine given was greater than appropriate. The large settlement reflected the nurse anesthetist's inadequacy to handle such a complicated situation.

Case 184. Physician's assistants and cast technicians may apply casts, but they are obligated to report to the patient's doctor when there is continuing pain, frequent change of cast, poor healing, or improper gait. If they fail to do so, the supervising physician will be at risk of liability for the bad result of having entrusted nonphysician assistants to make decisions that are beyond their scope of activity.

A physician's assistant had been entrusted to diagnose a patient with poor circulation and an acute ischemic foot. He failed to make the diagnosis, and a week was lost. As a result, the patient lost a leg. An expert witness was prepared to testify that timely diagnosis would have given the patient a 50/50 chance of saving the leg. Allowing the physician's assistant to diagnose such a case was substandard care. A large settlement was reached despite the patient's advanced age.

Case 185. A student nurse anesthetist was supervised by a physician's assistant who "specialized" in anesthesiology. Cardiac arrest and brain damage occurred. At the malpractice trial, it was held that a physician's assistant is not authorized by law to supervise a student nurse anesthetist. Therefore, the only issue for trial was whether the patient's injuries were caused by the student nurse anesthetist and, if so, the amount of damages.

Case 186. Student nurse anesthetists must be trained, but it is hard to imagine entrusting them with complex functions that, if done improperly, can harm the patient. In this case, an anesthesiologist was assisted by a certified nurse anesthetist and a student anesthetist. The latter was asked to turn off the nitrous oxide, but she extinguished the flow of oxygen instead. By the time the error was discovered, the patient suffered irreversible brain damage and died. Apparently there is very little that a student can be allowed to do without very close supervision.

Case 187. State hospital licensing regulations required a first assistant in surgery to be qualified to assist in major surgery in cases where there is unusual hazard to life. A bad result of a cholecystectomy raised the question of whether the surgical assistant was really qualified to serve as such in this major surgical procedure. It is a hospital obligation in granting staff privileges to delineate them, including designation as to serving as first assistant in surgery.

Case 188. The patient was a 10-year-old undergoing a splenectomy. He showed signs of shock, so the nurse summoned an intern who happened to be in his first week of service. He proved unable to do a cutdown, and this meant an undue delay in performing a blood transfusion, leading to cardiac arrest and brain damage. A huge award followed.

Inadequate Equipment; Poor Maintenance

One of the factors that distinguishes the developed world

from the developing is the respect for maintenance of mechanical equipment. Within the health care community, ill-maintained or inadequate equipment is not easily excused and can serve as the basis for malpractice suits when the malfunctioning equipment causes harm to patients.

Case 189. The siderails of a hospital bed gave way and the patient was hurt. It appeared that the rails were not intact and, had there been routine inspection, the defect would have been detected and presumably remedied.

Case 190. A baby was being returned home from a hospital in an ambulance. The incubator overheated and burned the child, causing some organ injury as well. The incubator did not have a controllable thermostat, nor was there a high-temperature alarm to warn the attendants. Because devices equipped with these safety measures were readily available and commonly in use, the defendant ambulance company was compelled to settle the claim for damages.

Case 191. A premature baby was in a special care nursery. At the age of 10 days, her pulse dropped to 40, and she needed to be resuscitated. It was found that the suction machine was not working, and, that somehow, the monitor alarm had been turned off. Some five to eight minutes of bradycardia occurred. The child recovered, although with residual effects. There was no malpractice claim, possibly because the infant was the offspring of an unsophisticated, unwed mother of disadvantaged background. The defects in the machinery, and especially the inexplicable turning off of the alarm, would have been difficult to explain away in defense of a lawsuit.

Case 192. While an indwelling plate in the patient's hip was being removed, three or four screws broke. It was necessary to remove these screws before a hip replacement could be accomplished. Unfortunately, a drill necessary to assist in removing the screws was unavailable. Therefore, a separate procedure was needed to remove the screws before the hip replacement could be scheduled, later than desired.

The patient, a nurse, should have been aware of the unnecessary delay caused by the missing drill. However, she was satisfied with payment of her wage loss without claiming damages caused by the negligence. Her loyalty to the institution and the doctors prevented a legitimate claim for suffering unnecessarily delayed remedial hip surgery because equipment was not ready for use.

Emergency Room: Casual Care

It is easy and often unfair to second-guess the doctors and other personnel who staff the hospital emergency room. There are, nevertheless, some situations that even laymen can readily identify as substandard professional care. These include not asking routine questions, such as those relating to medical history, allergies, medications being taken, or failure to do routine things such as standard diagnostic tests. The following examples of real cases are just a hint of the possibilities.

Case 193. A patient who had made a number of visits to the hospital emergency room complained of chest pain and also shoulder discomfort and radiating pain. His EKG proved to be abnormal, but he was sent home anyway. Apparently, the medical record indicating all his prior emergency room visits was never made available. The patient died of arterial disease. Since he left a wife and three fairly young children, the damages could have been immense. It would have been alleged that had his medical record been obtained, he would have proceeded to an arteriogram and possible bypass surgery. A very large settlement figure was accepted.

Case 194. What the emergency room physician does not know certainly can hurt him. In this case clearly he did not do a very thorough history because he did not learn that the patient previously had had cardiac bypass surgery. Consequently, the doctor was impressed by an unchanged EKG and assumed that the pain in the chest and left arm in the 65-year-old patient was esophageal in origin, subject to relief by taking oral lidocaine. The patient was relieved at first, but he died soon after returning home. When a medical consultant later reviewed the case and suggested that the patient should have been admitted to the hospital from the emergency room, the hospital prepared to settle the lawsuit filed by the patient's next of kin.

Case 195. A patient was left unattended in the emergency room for three hours, and then only an x-ray was taken. His death from pressure of blood around the brain created a presumption of negligent care so obvious that no medical expert testimony was needed. The court held that anyone applying common knowledge could judge whether the inattention to this patient constituted negligence.

Inattention to Patient's Needs or Behavior

Patients often make requests that are sensible and others that cannot be satisfied due to the patient's condition. In either instance, failure to pay attention can lead to liability.

Case 196. A stroke victim had left side paralysis but a nurse's aide allowed her to feed herself. At lunch the patient was left alone for 45 minutes with hot liquids. They spilled, and she suffered second- and third-degree burns on her insensitive side. The hospital's defense was that it was encouraging a stroke victim to learn how to take care of herself. Doing so without supervision or attendance was regarded as negligence and led to a significant settlement payment.

Case 197. A diathermy machine was set for 10 minutes. After eight minutes, the patient yelled for help because it was too hot. The practitioner's attendant placed an added towel between the patient and the machine. Therapy continued, and a third-degree burn resulted. Suit was filed. It would have been difficult to defend in the light of the inappropriate response of the attendant to the patient's clear and intense complaint. The attendant apparently was poorly trained, not very bright, and otherwise not qualified.

Case 198. An 88-year-old patient had been placed in a nursing home, where she appeared to have died of natural causes. The death certificate indicated a secondary cause of death to be dehydration and malnutrition. The patient's son, upon learning this, sued the attending physician. At issue was whether he should have ordered intravenous feeding when the patient would not eat. Or would it have been cruel and inhuman to have done so?

The jury verdict was for the doctor, perhaps in part because of the age and condition of the patient before she died. However, it would have been more prudent if the doctor, upon learning of the patient's refusal to eat, had determined whether the patient was competent and was exercising her right to refuse care and had brought the patient's son into the decision-making process.

Case 199. A very heavy patient, with I.V. tubing attached and requiring use of a walker, was authorized by his physician to have bathroom privileges. Despite close attention and personal assistance of a LVN attendant, the patient fell backwards upon entering the bathroom and broke an arm. Here the question is whether the physician should have granted bathroom privileges under the circumstances and whether the hospital nursing staff should have insisted that the doctor reconsider. A lay jury would question the common-sense justification for granting bathroom privileges in this situation.

Case 200. An obese, diabetic patient was to have various tests, some dependent on the results of others. The patient's vital signs deteriorated while the tests were in progress, but the nurse did not tell the attending physician or the next nurse coming on duty. As a consequence, the patient was virtually ignored, and the next morning he died. The hospital was sued because of the first nurse's poor observation and failure to communicate the patient's failing condition. A massive judgment resulted.

Case 201. Another example of failing to pay attention to the patient's needs and to communicate them to those who need to know is this catastrophe: When the patient was discharged from the emergency room, the accompanying nurse noted that the patient had become faint and dizzy. The nurse dutifully recorded this, but never told the treating physician. The patient recovered sufficiently to be driven home, where she became pale and clammy. She died that night. The doctor said he would have hospitalized the patient had he known of her dizziness because he suspected an ectopic pregnancy, but he did not suggest this to the nurse. This failure of communication between doctor and nurse contributed to the large settlement of the malpractice suit.

Case 202. When a patient with a suicidal background announces her intention to take her own life, attending personnel should pay attention. She should not be placed in an open ward from which she might easily escape to try suicide once again. In this case, the patient, a woman, was found perched on a freeway "waiting to be hit by a truck." She was saved, thus avoiding a wrongful death claim. The hospital would have been vulnerable to a malpractice action if she had sustained any harm.

Case 203. The patient succeeded in killing himself by jumping off a bridge after "eloping" from the psychiatric unit of a general hospital. The next of kin sued the hospital, contending that its personnel should have anticipated the escape, taken precautions to prevent it, and should have notified the police when the patient's absence was realized. At the trial, it was stated that the hospital would be liable for negligence if the patient's self-destructive behavior was involuntary due to his mental condition rather than a voluntary choice of one competent to so act. There was a verdict against the institution. Improved internal communications in the hospital might have helped to prevent the bad result.

Inexcusable Behavior of Hospital Personnel

There are some things that humans do that are understandable but unacceptable. Among hospital employees, who are often under strain or exhausted, forgetfulness or failure to act intelligently may be expected occasionally. Exposure to legal liability is not lessened, though, just because the employee may have good reason to be tired, angry, or inattentive. The standard of care, except in genuine emergencies such as natural disasters, is based upon the expected performance of a reasonable, prudent person in like circumstances with little or no concession to stressful personal circumstances. Hiring intelligent, well-trained employees who are emotionally stable is the first step toward avoiding malpractice because of personal defects of the individuals. This might have prevented the following unenviable and legally inexcusable situations.

Case 204. A dialysis nurse, provoked by a disruptive and abusive patient, removed the latter from the machine, leaving dialysis needles in the patient's arm. The patient proceeded to remove the needles himself. Consequently, he lost a lot of blood. He sued the hospital and, despite his own provocation of the nurse, won a judgment. There are ways of dealing with an abusive patient, but to do so abruptly and dangerously, as in this case, is not acceptable.

Case 205. Inattention of hospital personnel led to a very large award in this matter. There was inadequate monitoring of the pregnant patient during the childbirth period. There was no monitoring at all for two hours after administration of I.V. drip Pitocin, for five hours after the amniotic sac ruptured, or for three hours after amniotic fluid was found to be stained with meconium. Surely, this lack of attention was a violation of the hospital's own rules as well as substandard for the hospital community.

Case 206. A misplaced decimal point usually means human error. If it causes harm to a patient, defense of a malpractice claim is very difficult, if not impossible. Here the prescription was for .1 mg of Vincristine. The patient received 1 mg, a 10-fold overdose. There were severe and persistent neurological and other adverse effects, including bone marrow suppression and bladder difficulties. Personnel need to be constantly on the alert to avoid this easily committed mistake.

Case 207. The baby's bottle was heated by microwave. The nurse never checked the temperature of the contents in any way. The baby objected vehemently, but its complaints were ignored. It suffered a burned and scarred tongue and palate. A significant settlement figure resulted. Any layman would know that a few drops from the bottle should be tested on one's wrist or arm; no professional training is needed to apply the standard of care in this simple situation.

Case 208. The patient received injections that were repeatedly made at the very same spot on the hip, despite the patient's complaints of pain. As a result, there was necrosis of skin that took many months to heal. Had the personnel administering the shots consulted a physician when the patient complained about pain in the area of repeated injections, an instruction may have been given that would have avoided the serious injury and exposure to a malpractice claim.

Case 209. When hospital employees fail to observe an important house rule, subsequent bad results traceable to the omission make for an easily demonstrated case of malpractice. In this case, a baby suffering from diarrhea and related symptoms was brought into the emergency room for the second time in a few days. The nurse decided that the baby was stable and did not need to see a doctor, a violation of hospital rules calling for every pediatric patient in the emergency room to be seen by a physician. When the baby was returned once more, it suffered cardiac arrest and later died. An autopsy showed evidence of pneumonia and dehydration. The suit was tried, and a large verdict against the hospital resulted.

Case 210. The patient was admitted because of a possible kidney stone problem. The physician's first order for pain-relieving morphine was three times normal. The nurses failed to detect this and administered the overdose. The patient survived, and the physician corrected his error, prescribing the normal dosage for the next injection. Unfortunately, the attending nurse did not notice that the dosage had been reduced and gave the patient another triple overdose. The potential for injury to the patient, and the inability to defend the casual conduct of the hospital's nurses, meant the institution was extremely vulnerable to a malpractice action.

Case 210. During a resuscitation attempt on an 80-year-old patient, lidocaine was taken from the resuscitation cart. The nurse doing so did not notice that the dosage was 1000 ml rather than the usual 100 ml. The patient, upon receiving the substance, experienced cardiac arrest. Her family did not wish to have further resuscitation, so there wasn't any. They did not file a malpractice claim, since they were not disappointed with the results. Had the family felt differently, of course, this would have been a clear case of malpractice due to unobservant personnel.

Case 211. Another fortunate situation for the hospital was this one: A Crohn's disease patient already receiving morphine was supposed to get hyperalimentation solution. Instead, he was given one percent morphine sulfite solution, which caused him to be "jittery." There was no malpractice claim, but with the wrong medication being administered through neglect of hospital employees, the potential was present.

Case 212. When a patient received two mismatched components of a knee prosthesis, suit against the physician and the hospital followed. The subsequent surgery resulted in a fused knee. When the suit was tried, the doctor was found to be 80 percent responsible for the error in selecting the components and the hospital was held to be 20 percent liable. There was no need for the patient to produce any expert witness testimony, because selecting two different sizes of knee prosthesis components was negligence that an ordinary person could readily understand. Lack of customary alertness by hospital employees was recognized.

Case 213. When the blood sugar tests of an 84-year-old nursing home patient showed elevated levels, her physician was not informed. The patient was a diabetic. She went into shock and died after transfer to a hospital. The family filed no claim against the nursing home for reasons best known to them, but a negligence claim against the facility was quite possible under the circumstances.

Case 214. The obstetrician-gynecologist apparently was not anticipating complications for his patient; in any case he did not alert the hospital's nurses. They applied monitoring rather late, and until then they advised the doctor that things were going along normally. When the pediatrician entered the case, he was given an incorrect Apgar score by the nurses and was not told that it had been a premature birth. Both the obstetrician-gynecologist and the pediatrician were lulled into belief that the delivery and baby were normal. The child proved to be mentally retarded and partially blind. The doctors were vulnerable for not being at the hospital when they should have been. The hospital, whose nurses were so casual in their monitoring as to mislead the doctors, also was clearly at risk. The physicians and the hospital joined to settle the malpractice claim.

CHAPTER EIGHT

Reforms in the Legal System and Malpractice Insurance

THE FIRST LINE of defense against the malpractice threat is to reduce to a minimum the instances of professional negligence—that is, substandard performance that leads to undesired outcomes for patients. The next defensive barrier is insurance against the risks of practice. Then, if neither the number of malpractice claims nor the amount paid out per claim drops, the legal system is approached. The objective is alteration via tort reform to reduce certain features that are thought to be unfair to defendants. We are now seeing a wave of tort reform sweep across the nation. Patterned after the California experience, these tort reform measures are intended to cut the actual payout by reducing the dollar awards and converting lump sum compensation into annuity-type payments. Other kinds of changes in tort reform legislation are sought, but they have not made much difference in the incidence or cost of malpractice litigation where adopted.

One must realize that insurance problems are not unique to the health care field. In all areas of endeavor, the number of lawsuits filed has outstripped the population gain. We are a litigious nation. At the moment, about one personal injury suit is filed per year for every 15 Americans. The amounts awarded have leaped upward as well. Verdicts or settlements in excess of $1 million are commonplace—there were over 400 of them in 1984. Well publicized is the difficulty of some organizations in obtaining any insurance coverage from any source. Included in this group are cities, day care centers, sports equipment manufacturers, ice rinks, and some hospitals. Lawyers, engineers, and corporate board members, along with physicians in certain medical specialties, are finding coverage unaffordable or altogether unavailable. If obtained, the insurance protection is less comprehensive and more expensive than previously.

Part of the problem may well be the attitude of jurors—who are intended to be a cross section of the community—that deserving injured parties should be compensated, sometimes irrespective of the rules of law that delineate what constitutes negligence. If the defendant is a large corporation, a presumably rich hospital or doctor, or an expectedly well-insured party, jurors seem to have no reluctance in holding for the plaintiff—and in substantial amounts. Compounding the problem is that the litigation system itself is very time consuming and expensive. That adds to the total cost of the malpractice risk business.

Insurance Industry Objectives

Some commercial insurers have mounted a national campaign to create public awareness of the costs, both in dollars and to society, of the rampant increase in personal injury suit litigation and related awards. In addition, they are attempting to influence legislatures to enact reform legislation. The objectives are to narrow the definition of liability; to put limits on the dollar amounts that may be awarded; require the loser to pay the winner's court costs and legal fees; restrict the plaintiffs' lawyers contingency fees; all but eliminate punitive damages; curtail damages for pain and suffering; and encourage more mediation and binding arbitration.

In an appeal to the public, one national insurance brokerage firm has placed advertisements telling of the effects of high malpractice insurance premiums, including doctors switching to less risky procedures or specialties or retiring early. One in 4 of all doctors and 6 out of 10 obstetricians have been sued, the ad states. Plaintiffs are said to be zealously engaged in a "litigation lottery." Therefore, tort reform is a must, the message concludes.

Medical malpractice insurers have not carried out an organized campaign for these reforms, however.

INCIDENCE AND COST OF INSURANCE

Irrespective of tort reform, the experience in recent years— 1975 to 1983—is that the number of suits against physicians has tripled, the average settlement reportedly reaching $330,000; premiums for malpractice insurance coverage were 10 percent less than the amounts paid out in liability claims. Investment income kept most of the malpractice carriers in the business, however, and premiums rose more slowly than actuarial losses during this period.

Nevertheless, the General Accounting Office has estimated that from 1975 to 1985 medical malpractice insurers earned in excess of 1.6 billion dollars. It further reports that from 1983 to 1985 total malpractice insurance costs for American hospitals increased by 53 percent; for physicians, the increase was 100 percent. Other sources show frequency of malpractice claims during the same period rose 53 percent for hospitals, 18 percent for physicians while average paid claims were up 51 percent for hospitals and 31 percent for physicians.

Justifying its premiums and rate increases, one major carrier has advised its insured physicians that the average general or family practitioner's 1986 premium comes to only about 46 cents per patient visit. To the average surgeon (class V), the rates amount to $41 per surgical procedure, while obstetricians average $167 per delivery. So described, the costs of malpractice insurance seem to be affordable. But these national averages do not reflect great variations from one area to another. Broken down by state, average annual malpractice premiums for general practitioners who do major surgery range from $5,640 in Arkansas to $39,200 in California (Los Angeles). For many specialties, the premiums are much higher.

For hospitals, insurance coverage tends to be available, subject to substantial deductibles and unrealistically low maximum coverage limits. The reinsurance market no longer is eager to cover the excess layers of protection that hospitals need. Hospital coverage often requires the institution to have a functioning loss prevention or risk management program and mandatory malpractice coverage for each medical staff member. The premium per hospital bed (for $1 million per claim and $3 million annual aggregate of claims) for 1986 charged by a major carrier ranges from $6,000 in Detroit to $2,374 in Cleveland, among the largest cities. The national average comes to $1,495 per bed, with Arkansas at the low end and West Virginia at the top.

Medical Tort Reforms

What reforms are sought by the commercial insurance industry? They seek limits on noneconomic (pain and suffering) damages; ending double payment of damages by counting collateral sources; restricting plaintiffs' attorneys' contingent fees; penalties for attorneys who bring "frivolous" malpractice suits; shorter periods during which suit may be brought; ending "deep-pocket" liability of jointly liable defendants whose share of culpability is small; required structured payments or periodic payment of damages, whether awarded or agreed to by settlement; and eliminating or limiting possible punitive damages.

Most of these objectives have been enacted into law in California affecting medical malpractice cases. Therefore, examination of the experience there can help to predict which of the reforms will save money and which will be disadvantageous to patients who really are victims of malpractice.

In California, damages for pain and suffering in malpractice suits are limited by statute to $250,000. In cases in which pain and suffering rather than past and future medical expenses and lost earnings are the large components of total damages, the cap at $250,000 has saved the defendants and their carriers a considerable sum. California's average jury award in 1984, 10 years after the law was enacted, was only 41 percent of the national average, whereas a decade earlier it had been in the top 20 percent. This may represent a 10 to 30 percent reduction in potential judgments, especially in settlement amounts.

Elimination of collateral source payments is not absolutely required under California law. However, the jury may be told by the defense that the patient has already received health insurance benefits, workers' compensation, and other such benefits that the patient does not need to pay back. Undoubtedly, this helps the defense, but it is impossible to know how much attention the jury has paid to this provision when it calculates a single figure for compensatory damages. Plaintiffs' attorneys, faced with a case where most damages already have been paid for by a third party, and the physical injury is modest, may well refrain from pursuing a malpractice case because of this provision.

Limiting the plaintiffs' attorneys' contingent fees, at first consideration, should put more of the award money into the victorious patients' pockets. In California, the plaintiff's attorney is allowed a maximum of 40 percent of the first $50,000 awarded, 33.3 percent of the next $50,000, 25 percent of the next $100,000, and only 10 percent of anything over $200,000. Thus, in small cases the fee is conventional, but for the big-ticket suits the attorneys' reward is much reduced. A million-dollar award brings an attorney's fee of $140,000, which some plaintiffs' counsel claim does not cover the cost of bringing the matter to trial. A survey done for the Rand Corporation has indicated that, despite this disincentive, there seems to be no reduction in the number of malpractice suits filed in California. The trial lawyers complain that worthy but poor patients will be unable to persuade competent malpractice lawyers to take their cases when the contingent fee is so limited by law. Since the number of cases filed is not dropping, the plaintiffs evidently are not wanting for attorneys to represent them. Nor are these attorneys so inadequate that their clients are getting poor results for their efforts. More likely, the attorney is motivated to settle rather than go to trial when the contingent fee for the marginal gain is only 10 percent.

The frivolous suit penalty has not been part of the California tort reform legislation package. Rules of court in many jurisdictions permit judges to impose such penalties. They rarely do because the privilege of bringing suit is considered to be a customary right of Americans, and judges are not inclined to interfere with the free exercise of this liberal view of our society. On the other hand, judges always have had the authority to reduce damage awards that are well in excess of the proof or that seem motivated by the jurors' passion. Occasionally, a large damage award is reduced or set aside.

The statute of limitations in malpractice cases in California was set at one to three years for adults and at eight years for most minors, an apparent tightening up of the previous periods during which suits could be filed. However, the courts have applied the "discovery" rule, so that the patient has a year after discovering that he was the possible victim of malpractice before his suit is barred. And if the health care practitioner or hospital withheld information so that the patient could not have known of the malpractice cause of his injury, then not until that discovery by the patient—no matter how long—does the clock start to run on the time limit. Not many more malpractice suits have been barred by the new statute of limitations than before, inasmuch as judges prefer to find a way for plaintiffs to have their day in court.

The joint and several liability exposure for nonecomonic damages has been diminished in California as a result of voters' approval of a 1986 initiative on the state ballot. The pain and suffering component of damages, as apportioned by the jury among a number of co-defendants, will be fixed as to each such defendant. If, for example, an uninsured doctor is found 90 percent liable and a hospital is only 10 percent responsible for the damages, the hospital may be obliged to pay 100 percent of the medical expenses and loss of income but only 10 percent of the pain and suffering award. How much of a saving to the malpractice defense community will result from this partial restoration of fairness is not known at this writing. The new law may discourage litigation in some cases where pain and suffering is the major component of damages, where the primary defendant is judgment proof, and where the deep-pocket defendant is protected by the limit on liability to its own percentage of guilt.

Periodic payment of the damage award is required in California if malpractice damages exceed $50,000. This constitutes a very definite saving to the insurance carriers covering the malpractice defendant. Instead of making a large cash payment in a lump sum, the carrier arranges to make the installment payments through an annuity. The present value of future payments is always less than the sum to be paid out because the lump sum can be invested and will produce earnings over time. Therefore, a much smaller sum need be invested in the annuity than the amount of the total payment. Thus, in cases involving large judgments, this provision of the tort reform law, plus the limit on damages for pain and suffering, has reduced the total payout on behalf of malpractice defendants. In the cases in which the damages are modest, however, the tort reform provisions do not have much impact.

Punitive damages have not been a major element in malpractice damage awards heretofore, and there have been no statutory changes concerning them in California as yet.

It appears, then, that only two of the tort reform measures produce significant savings, and then only in cases of large awards. The rest of the provisions either produce modest savings, no savings, or the benefits have not been ascertainable. Nevertheless, doctors and hospitals in California have been able to purchase insurance at premiums that would have been perhaps 40 percent greater without the reform legislation.

CHANNELING OF INSURANCE

One of the problems in defending malpractice claims arising at hospitals is that the doctor defendant and hospital defendant usually are insured by different companies. A defense strategy is for each defendant, in its own interest, to blame the other but thereby make it easier for the plaintiff to prove that somebody committed malpractice. If all defendants were insured by the same carrier, this embarrassment could be eliminated. Where a large health maintenance organization has its own hospitals as well as its contracting physicians who see the HMO's members there, a unified insurance program is attainable. It should be less expensive than if all doctors and hospitals were individually insured and defended, and it should end the gratuitous proof of liability by the defendants themselves.

The term "channeling" has been coined to describe a program of coverage of the hospital and its primary medical staff members under the same insurance policy. But in this arrangement, very large limits of coverage are required, more than may be available on the market. Cooperation between doctors and hospital at a higher level than previously prevailed also is needed. There are numerous problems to be overcome before channeling can become popular, including disinclination of some doctors to be bound to one hospital and resistance of smaller malpractice carriers who will lose out, in the competition, to a single insurer covering the hospital and all of its most active staff members.

Litigation, the American Lottery

Tinkering with tort laws may help to place a cap on certain

damages, but it cannot remedy the fundamental defects of the American legal system. It is a game of combat that is elaborate, expensive, and time consuming. Lawyers on either side absorb as much as two-thirds of the money spent on malpractice insurance. After deducting administrative costs and profit, if any, of the insurance companies, it is evident that the successful claimant gets only a small slice of the insurance premium pie. Those who suffer severe injuries but have difficulty in proving malpractice may go uncompensated, while the same situation and a slight change of facts may bring a large award. Many deserving claimants are unpaid because their claim isn't big enough to warrant suit. Others go uncompensated because they did not realize, or did not realize soon enough, that the poor result of medical care they experienced may have been because of medical negligence. Ironically, the very big awards that so distort the insurance premiums are rarely enjoyed by the severely injured party; the healthy relatives usually get to use the money.

Alternative Systems

It would be possible to replace the present system with a no-fault system resembling workers' compensation, as has been done in New Zealand, but such a system would not be really feasible in this country because of the cost. We know now that far more compensable events occur than are reflected in actual malpractice claims. Even if the payment schedule were modest in a no-fault program, as in workers' compensation programs, the total cost would be far more than at present. It would be a fairer system, but it would increase the already burdensome cost of health care in the United States. If a national health insurance program were adopted and virtually all doctors and hospitals were participants, one feature could be either a no-fault program of limited, affordable benefits, or a streamlined claims system somewhat like the one employed by Social Security for disputed disability claims, using hearing officers and avoiding the court system. But adoption of a national health insurance program, itself more expensive than the existing nonorganized system, is an extremely remote possibility given the already record-setting federal deficit and the current national mood.

Just as remote is the likelihood of the United States adopting the Canadian legal system, in which judges, not juries, resolve malpractice claims and set the amount of damages, and in which lawyers, in most provinces, may not take cases on a contingency fee basis. These simple reforms are unlikely for a long time in any state in this country simply because American trial lawyers, with some support from the organized bar, constitute a formidable lobby.

Arbitration is a procedural reform, taking cases out of the courts and simplifying the hearing itself, as well as shortening the period of the dispute and lowering some of the costs. For the moment, it is contractual; that is, the parties must agree to it. A few HMOs have been able to enforce their compulsory, binding arbitration requirements in contracts with their members, but individual doctors and hospitals have been less successful.

The use of mandatory mediation or review panels prior to being allowed to bring suit has been of only minor help in discouraging malpractice lawsuits and promoting settlements. Some state statutes requiring these pretrial hearings have been held unconstitutional, in part for delaying plaintiffs access to court.

It appears, then, that we will have to live with some variant of the present legal system for the foreseeable future. If thousands of automobile accident cases are still being decided by the same legal system designed for the horse and buggy era of Victorian England, what are the chances for an efficient, just, and affordable arrangement for resolving malpractice claims?

CHAPTER NINE

Some Parting Advice

IF THE REALITY is that we are going to have the present tort law system, with disputes ultimately resolved in the courts, for a long time to come, then we must do our best to use it to our favor, or learn to avoid its more punishing aspects. Avoidance of preventable bad results of medical treatment and adopting appropriate defensive practices are measures that are available right now.

Who would know how to avoid malpractice claims better than the plaintiffs' lawyers who make a living bringing such suits? When asked to advise physicians on how to avoid malpractice litigation, a representative group of these attorneys, including physicians-turned-lawyers, had these suggestions:

1. Do a truly complete history and physical examination.
2. Try to avoid making questionable professional decisions by telephone.
3. Come to see the patient in the hospital when called unless you are absolutely certain of the diagnosis and/or treatment.
4. When in doubt about what to do, ask yourself how you or your family members would like to be treated if you or they were the patient.

5. Work at appearing to be, and actually being, a sympathetic, caring practitioner; patients are reluctant to sue a doctor whom they think is genuinely concerned about them. However, unctuous deportment, easily seen through, won't do.
6. Do not unrealistically heighten the patient's expectations prior to surgery or other treatment; confidence is desirable, but overconfidence of the doctor and patient, followed by a bad result, invites suit.
7. Good communications between physician and patient are the best preventive. This means a full explanation, by the doctor himself, to the patient as to what is wrong, what is to be done, how much it will hurt, what it will cost, how long it will take to recuperate, what are the risks, what are the alternatives, and what might happen if no treatment is undertaken. Try to make sure that the patient really understands.
8. Complete documentation is essential for defense since, if it is not recorded, it may be assumed not to have occurred. Contents of telephone conversations also should be noted in the records, including oral instructions and warnings given.
9. If a patient expresses significant fears, misconceptions, suspicions, or anxieties, a note should describe this in the record along with the doctor's explanations given to clarify and correct the patient's misunderstandings.
10. Careful and complete records often can prevent malpractice suits even when the patient's care has ended in a bad result.
11. In obtaining informed consent, the physician should include a copy in the hospital medical record and note how consent was acquired.
12. Anesthesiologists—a high-risk group—should remain in the operating room throughout the procedure and until the patient is taken safely from the room.
13. A belated decision to do a cesarean section often means

liability if the baby emerges defective, so timely decisions should be a high priority.

14. The informed consent process is intended to allow the patient to make his own decision; it is not just a procedural obligation and personal nuisance for physicians.

15. Honesty toward the patient is essential; if the doctor knows there has been or suspects there will be a bad result, he should advise the patient in a timely manner. Tardiness in this regard is suspect.

16. Communications between doctors and nurses should be as clear as possible. If written instructions are given, abbreviations should be avoided unless they are standard and universally understood.

Added to the list should be the caution to practice defensive medicine, especially if the patient is a stranger, possibly a drug addict, or a down-and-outer whose hope for financial salvation is a vexatious malpractice claim. And maintain adequate malpractice insurance coverage, preferably from a large, old, financially sound and stable carrier.

INDEX

A

Abandonment
  examples of, 91
Abortion
  See Pregnancy
Abram, Morris B., 38
Addiction, 86, 113, 125
  and practitioners, 97
Adult incompetent, 35, 60
  mental patient, 64–65
  See also Mental patient
Alcoholism, 97–98
Allergic reaction, 83, 126
Ambulance chasers, 20
American Medical Association, 99
American Psychiatric Association, 99
Amniocentesis, 42–43
  and failing to order, 80
  and fetal death, 56–57
Amputation, 66
Anesthesia
  and childbirth, 82
  and claims, 8–9, 15, 152
  and equipment, 120
  by nurse anesthetist, 129–130
  and untrained attendant, 93
Anger, 23–24, 37
Arkansas
  insurance in, 143–144
Arthritis, 86–87
Attorneys
  See Lawyers
Autopsy, 102, 113

B

Billing
  disputed, 22, 25
  and follow-up, 90
  and inability to pay, 92–94, 103, 123–125
Birth control
  IUD, 49
  pills, 44–45
  See also Pregnancy
Births
  brain-damaged, 116–117, 128
  defective, 51, 153
  dying in childbirth, 82, 129

and hemophilia, 78
and non-English-speaking
   patient, 67
stillbirth, 56–57, 79, 128
See also Birth control,
   Pregnancy
Brain
   damage, 116–117, 120–121
   surgery, 85–86
Burn patients, 93

C

California
   insurance statistics in, 8, 143
   and reform laws, 4, 7–8, 141, 144–148
Canada
   legal system of, 150
Cancer
   breast, 50, 63, 74–75, 80–81
   delayed diagnosis of, 39–40, 69, 77–78, 84
   disclosing, 59
   and Pap test, 46–47, 80
Cardiology
   and medical history information, 83, 132
   and misprescribing, 81
   and records, 115
Cleveland
   insurance in, 144
Communication
   and consent, 32–34
   and dissatisfaction, 23–24
   between doctor and nurse, 135, 153
   non-English, 66–67
   between physicians, 59–60, 63, 65
   as prevention, 20–21, 25, 152

and technical language, 28, 34, 56
Concealment, 57
   possibility of, 49
Concern
   as a preventive, 22, 71
Confidence
   in physician, 56, 152
Confidentiality, 52
   breach of, 107
   and personnel, 101
   psychiatric, 67–68
Credentialing, 70
   and malpractice prevention, 108–110
Crohn's disease, 85, 139

D

Deception—See Concealment
Deep-pocket principle, 3–4, 144, 147
Dental care
   and anesthesia, 93
   and consent, 60
   surgical, 70–71
Detroit
   insurance in, 144
Diabetics, 134–135
   instructions about, 112–113
   misprescribing for, 71
   and referrals, 85
Diagnosis
   absentee, 113, 151
   delayed, 39, 69, 75
   incorrect, 71, 83–84
   by personnel, 101, 129
   and psychosomatics, 79
   and tests, 73–76
   unrevealed, 47
Dilantin, 51

INDEX

Disability benefits
  and testing, 83
Discharge
  premature, 123–125
Discipline of physicians
  by hospital, 85–86, 107–108
  impaired or incompetent, 97
  and risk management, 106
Disillusionment, 23–24
Dissatisfaction
  See Satisfaction
Down's syndrome, 42–43
  and amniocentesis, 80
Drugs
  abuse of, 97–98, 110
  experimental, 40
  and medical history
    information, 83
  misprescribing, 71, 81, 94
  Pitocin, 59–60
  Prednisolone, 86
  Provera, 80
  risks of, 47–48, 51, 62–63
  side effects of, 23, 36, 46,
    53, 125–126
  and telephone prescribing,
    86–87, 94–95

E

Education
  drug, 110
  and doctors-in-training, 42
  of patients, 33, 45
  of personnel, 106
Elective surgery, 39
Emergencies, 90
  and consent, 31, 35
  and inadequately trained
    personnel, 128

and rejecting patients, 91–93,
  123–125
substandard care in, 132–133
and tests, 74–76
Equipment
  failure, 55
  improper use of, 119–121
  inadequate, 130–132
Errors
  admitting to, 54, 56
Eutonyl, 46
Examination
  thoroughness of, 73–83
Experimental treatment, 72
  See also Drugs, Surgery

F

Fallibility, 28–29
  of physician, 37
Florida
  laws for hospitals, 106–107
Follow-up
  failing to, 87, 89
  and patient satisfaction, 22,
    26
  postabortion, 86

G

Gastroenterology
  and timely referrals, 85
Genetic counseling, 51
Gynecology
  See Birth control, Births,
    Pregnancy

H

Health Maintenance
  Organizations (HMOs), 148,
  150
Heart
  See Cardiology
Hemophilia, 78
Hippocratic oath, 99
Historical perspective, 2
Hypochondriacs, 23
  and drugs, 125
  nontreatment of, 91
Hysterectomy, 50, 101
  on pregnant patient, 82
  unconsented, 58, 60
  unnecessary, 44, 53

I

Impairment, 98-99
Informed refusal, 35-36
Instruments
  See Equipment
Insurance, 3, 109, 141, 153
  channeling, 148
  discontinued, 100
  and government, 108,
    142-148
  increased, 64
  lack of, 54, 92-94, 103,
    123-125, 142
  national health, 149-150
  St. Paul Fire and Marine,
    9-17
  statistics, 8, 141, 143-144
Investigational procedures
  informing patients of, 49
  surgery, 39-40

J

Juries
  and witnesses, 34-35

L

Lawyers
  ambulance chasers, 20
  fees, 6-7, 145, 149
Laws
  Canadian, 150
  in California, 4, 7-8, 141,
    144-145
  for Florida hospitals,
    106-107
  Health Care Quality
    Improvement Act of
    1986, 107-108
  reform, 141-148
  statute of limitations, 121
Licensing, 108-110
  improper, 127-130

M

Malpractice
  avoiding litigation, 151
  defined, 18-19
Mastectomy
  and treatment choice, 50
  unnecessary, 54
Medical history information,
    82-83
  to avoid litigation, 151
  in emergency rooms, 132
Medicare, 124-125
Medication
  See Drugs
Mental patients, 31

and confidentiality, 67–68
and plastic surgery, 70
psychosomatics, 79
refusing medication, 52
and spousal consent, 64–65
See also Adult incompetent
Minors
and consent, 35

N

Neurology
and timely referrals, 84
New Zealand
compensation in, 149

O

Obesity
failed surgery for, 69
and inhospital behavior, 134–135
jejunoileal shunt for, 44
Obstetrics
See Birth control, Births, Pregnancy
Office staff
and call screening, 22, 27
delegating care to, 93–94
entrusting responsibility to, 101–103
Ophthalmology, 71
eyesight loss, 83
and glaucoma test, 74
and harmful testing, 87
and untrained assistants, 93
Orthopedics
referrals to, 85
surgery, 8

P

Part-time practitioners, 6
Pediatrics, 83, 115, 138
and referrals, 84
Peer review, 110–111
and confirmation, 117
and criticism, 126–127
Personnel
and inappropriate delegation, 101–103
unacceptable care by, 136–139
Peyronie's disease, 71
Physician's Desk Reference, 51
and misprescribing, 72
Pitocin, 59
Podiatry, 117, 126
Postoperative complications, 9, 15
and abandonment, 94
See also Follow-up
Poverty
and inability to pay for care, 92–94, 103, 123–125
and lawyers, 145–146
and refusing tests, 46
and unconsented surgery, 57
Prednisolone, 86
Pregnancy
aborted, 41, 80, 86, 94
and amniocentesis, 42–43
high-risk, 79, 85, 139
and rubella testing, 81
and unauthorized treatment, 59–60
See also Births
President's Commission for the Study of Ethical Problems in Medicine and Biomedical Behavioral Research, 37

Privacy
  See Confidentiality
Prolixin, 53
Prosthesis
  mismatched, 139
Psychiatry
  and confidentiality, 67–68
  and parental consent, 59
  and psychosomatics, 79
  and sex with patients, 99–100
  and suicide, 135–136
  See also Mental patient
Psychosomatics
  and testing, 79

Q

Qualifications
  and impairment, 98–99
  inadequate, 127–130
  of physicians, 69–70, 108

R

Radiation therapy
  and negligence, 95
  risks of, 48, 82–83
Records
  of consent, 32–33, 61, 152
  of explanations, 35, 39, 45, 63
  falsified, 65–66, 117–118
  of instructions, 26–28, 152
  late entry of, 62
  of maintenance, 127
  omissions in, 115
  of patient requests, 61
  of previous work, 126–127
  of tests, 76–77
  of warnings, 116–126

Referrals
  confusion about, 23
  and consent, 41
  late, 75, 84–86
  and physician communications, 59–60, 63, 65
  See also Specialists
Reform
  See Laws
Relief physicians, 114
Research, 8
  of dissatisfaction, 23–24
  and lawyers, 6–7
  surveys, 5, 145
Restraints, 118–119
Risk, 118–119
  of absentee diagnosing, 112–113
  and consent, 31, 34, 36
  conveying, 24, 27, 40, 62–63
  genetic, 51
  management, 3, 105–106
  of transfer, 124
  unrevealed, 42–44, 48, 49

S

St. Paul Fire and Marine Insurance Co., 9–17
Satisfaction
  dissatisfaction, 23–25
  and follow-up, 22
  and informed consent, 38
Senility
  of physicians, 98
Sex
  with patients, 99
  treatment for dysfunction, 71
Side effects, 24
  discussing, 34
  of drugs, 23, 46–47, 125–126

unrevealed, 42–43
  of vaccines, 36
Specialists, 40
  as expert witnesses, 72
  failure to consult, 83–86, 117
  timely referral to, 75
  See also Referrals
Spouse
  consent of, 60, 64–65, 67
  and sexual dysfunction, 71
  surviving, 75, 95
Statistics
  of awards, 5, 7, 143
  of insurer, 9–17
  of litigation, 141–142
  by year, 5
Sterilization, 63–64, 66–67
  See Birth control
Stroke
  and inattention, 133
Social Security
  and claim disputes, 149–150
Substance abuse
  by practitioners, 97–98
  See also Addictions,
    Alcoholism, Drugs
Suicide, 68
  and vulnerability to
    malpractice, 135–136
Surgery, 55
  brain, 85–86
  dental, 70–71
  and equipment, 120–123
  errors, 112
  exploratory, 39–40, 49
  first assistant in, 130
  general, 8
  by "ghost" surgeon, 91
  inability to pay for, 92
  mastectomy, 50, 54
  pediatric, 83–84
  plastic, 70
  unconsented, 57–58
  urgency of, 54

T

Tardive dyskinesia, 52
Telephone practice, 26–27, 151
  and medication prescribing,
    87, 94–95
  records of, 152,
  and staff, 101
Tests
  double-checking, 76
  harmful, 87
  inadequate, 73–83
  Pap, 46
  and psychosomatics, 79
  side effects of, 43
  See also Risks
Thorazine, 53
Transfusions, 114
Transplants
  and testing, 74
Treatment alternatives, 42–43,
    45
  for mastectomy, 50
Trust, 25
  and disappointment, 23–24
Truth, 22–23

V

Vasectomy, 92–93
Veterans Administration, 65
  problem physicians in,
    109–110

W

Warning of risks, 38–41, 152
  with drugs, 62–63, 125–126
  by equipment, 120–121
  by psychotics, 67–68
West Virginia
  insurance in, 144

Witnesses
   and consent, 33–35
   expert, 72, 79, 129
   professional, 18

X

X-rays, 73, 84
   absence of, 74–75
   barium, 79
   chest, 87
   by patient request, 78–79
   preparing for, 46
   and unaccounted surgical
      instruments, 122